WOMEN
and
POWER

HOW FAR CAN WE GO?

WOMEN
—and—
POWER

HOW FAR CAN WE GO?

Nancy Kline

BBC BOOKS

For Edelweiss

Published by BBC Books,
a division of BBC Enterprises Limited,
Woodlands, 80 Wood Lane, London W12 0TT

First Published 1993

© Nancy Kline 1993

ISBN 0 563 36449 1

Designed by

Cover photograph © BBC Enterprises (John Jefford)

Set in Century Old Style by Phoenix Photosetting, Chatham, Kent
Printed and bound in Great Britain by Clays Ltd, St Ives plc
Cover printed by Clays Ltd, St Ives plc

Contents

Part 3: Going Into Action

Part 4: Reminders

Author's Note

I have told many people's stories here. The details and conclusions are authentic, but I have used pseudonyms to honour the confidentiality between us.

Acknowledgements

For detailed help in writing this book I am particularly grateful to Christopher Spence, Amy Cassidy, Margit Birge, Sara Collier, Francis Fitzgerald, Merl Glasscock, Rosalind Hawkes, Vanessa Helps, Jennifer Johnson, Augusta McCabe, Nancy Owens, my copy editor Kelly Davis, and at BBC Books my editor Deborah Taylor, and my commissioning editor, Suzanne Webber.

I also thank the many, many other women who have contributed to this book and who have been of support to me in writing it.

Introduction

About ten years ago I was sitting at the kitchen table with my mother. That was her favourite place, I think, because outside the kitchen window were the wide open skies of West Texas. She said she could think best when she could see a long, long way. Also, not surprisingly, that was where she and I had our best conversations.

On that particular late afternoon, we were talking about women. We didn't often talk about women. And that worried me because I knew that during this visit, I wanted to tell her that I had decided to resign from my secure position as director of the school I had co-founded and focus my work on women's empowerment. I was afraid, as I had been most of my life, of overturning her peace.

But I had reached that point between us where it was harder not to tell than to tell. I don't know what I expected from her, really, but I was shaking. I suppose her life as a wife and mother, and her choice to speak out only on issues that would not alarm my father, had made me think that she would sigh at the thought of my joining the public debate about women. Now sighing might not seem like much to be afraid of, but from my mother it signified profound disapproval and was too often the apparent precursor to unexplained illnesses. Whenever one of us behaved in an unconventional way, she seemed to end up in hospital under an oxygen tent. So I did not approach this conversation blithely.

But on that afternoon, something wonderful happened between us. I can't account for it except to say that I probably had not really known my mother before that moment. Probably, like so many daughters, I had made the wrong assumptions based on her outward activity. Until that moment I had not realized that every woman, beneath the co-operative veneer of her life, understands and loathes her oppression.

We were sitting at that round wooden table, talking in treasured fragments as we often did while preparing dinner. I wanted to say it well. I wanted her to understand how much I wanted women's lives to be better and how much I wanted women to lead our world.

I wanted to explain that I was exploring sexism from the inside out, working with women to remove the barriers inside that hold us back. I wanted to tell her that I could see the pain and the power in the eyes of women and the huge possibilities at our fingertips, and that I wanted to help women remove the barriers between ourselves and our power, to. look at our excellence, to squint into the blinding light of what we could do if we did not hold back, to stop saying, 'Be careful,' and start saying, on a daily basis, 'Yes, you can. Do it. I will support you'. I wanted her to agree that women must now stop hiding from their excellence.

I wondered what she would think of the idea that our progress as women is measured not only in our political gains, but also in the decreasing amount of time each day we spend as victims. And I wondered if she would agree that if we stayed true to our culture as women, men might eventually follow us, unable to resist because the light ahead was bright and the journey would be so much fun.

I wanted to reassure her, too. I did not want her to think that I had decided to protest by chaining my braless body to the White House gate. But I also wanted her to understand that I was committed to women. (Anyway, it was her fault because every time I had stamped my foot as a child, she had said that in another era I would have been an Emmeline Pankhurst or a Susan B. Anthony. As a child, I hadn't known who on earth those women were, but I had noticed that, as she said it, she was smiling.) So I told her.

And she was amazing.

She listened all the way through. She did not interrupt me. She did not sigh.

She got up, walked over to the stove, turned up the heat, and said nothing until the oil was crackling in the pan. As she dropped the floured chicken into the oil, the noise becoming just loud enough to keep anyone else in the family from hearing her, she whispered in my ear, 'When I was a girl, women did not have the vote. Fighting for women's suffrage was a huge challenge. But it was easy compared to what you are trying to do. This stage of liberation is the hardest – don't give up.'

This book is about what has happened since that conversation. For me these past ten years have been a time of listening to women. In many parts of the world I have gathered together with women in thinking groups, in workshops, in meetings and in private consultations. I hear women asking themselves relentlessly, 'How far can we go? Are there limits to what we can do in the world? How much power can we take in public life and in our personal lives? Can we really lead in numbers proportionate to our population, and if we can, can we lead the world better than male-conditioned leaders have had to do? Can we decide to exercise full choice in our circumstances, have full say over our own bodies, and bring full female enfranchisement into politics, business', work, religion, and home? Can we really remake society so that it doesn't hurt people?'

As far as I can tell, women almost everywhere, and from many identities and backgrounds, are asking these questions.

I believe that the answer to all these questions is *Yes*. Yes, we can go as far as we can see – and farther. We can do all the things we can conceive of doing, and more. We can show the world a new kind of leadership. Women, I believe, can do anything. We can, that is, if we can overcome the barriers that stand between us and our power.

Barriers come in two forms:

1 External oppression – laws, policies and structures that keep women from power.
2 Internal oppression – sexist conditioning that causes us to hold *ourselves* back.

Both types of barriers are real. Both are deadly. Both need our understanding and committed vigilance.

Women are moving forward steadily against external oppression. We now need to make new gains against internal oppression.

In my work with women of many ages I see just how tightly we are bound by these internal barriers. Sometimes they have grabbed us by the throat and terrified us. Sometimes they have flung themselves, desperate, at our feet and left us feeling guilty. Other times they have screamed at us from the shore and changed our course. They have pulled us aside with a whisper and a wink and promised to take care of us.

In order for women to have the lives we want and to lead the world the way we want, we will have to be more intelligent than the barriers. We will have to be more intelligent than the seductive voices in our own heads that keep us believing we have chosen the limits freely. We will have to be clever enough to beware when oppression looks and feels like freedom and in those dangerous moments turn with a flourish back to our real selves.

In this book I have begun to face what it will take to remove these internal barriers to our power. I have come to believe that the barriers will not budge until we set up the right conditions under which to *think clearly* about our lives, boldly and for ourselves, every day. Action of any kind is only as good as the *thinking* behind it, and so in order for us to act from the centre of our power, we must change the thinking that has been beneath our powerless actions.

THE THINKING ENVIRONMENT

If action is only as good as the thinking behind it, thinking is only as good as the way people behave with each other. Some types of behaviour help us to think. Other types of behaviour stop us from thinking. We need to know the difference and begin practising with each other the kind of interaction that will help us think powerfully.

I have called these conditions a *Thinking Environment*, and have identified ten components of behaviour that create this kind of environment. I have suggested how we can turn our places of work, our families, our meetings and our relationships into thinking environments, so that as we take the lead, the world we are leading will change.

Throughout this book I use the word *thinking* to describe the vast, multi-faceted process of intelligence that includes feelings, creativity, speculation and intuition as well as cognition, analysis and computation. Thinking in this context is the *full* use of the human mind, and a thinking environment is the behaviour or circumstance that allows the mind to work fully.

THE THINKING PARTNERSHIP

As women seriously consider going beyond our current limits, we will need daily thinking time and encouragement from other women in order not to stray from a self-chosen course of empowerment. One of the principles of leadership I see verified over and over again is that people should: 'Increase the amount of support in their life proportionate to the amount of leadership they take.' I recommend a daily structure of practical leadership support called a *Thinking Partnership*. This is an equal exchange of listening time between two people specifically intended to remove internal barriers, plan next steps, and appreciate each other.

Since 1985 my work with women has been called Project 2020. I have called it that because our goal is for women to be leading proportionate to our numbers (52 per cent) by the year 2020. But implicit in that goal is that leaders change by becoming experts in creating a thinking environment.

The catalyst for Project 2020 was a magazine article I read while I was flying to Alaska. (Important things always seem to happen to me when I am flying to Alaska. The glacial fields of Western Canada seem to say that there is time to think big.)

The writer of the article had said that the main difficulty in getting women into leadership was lack of money for women's political campaigns. But as I read, I began to think about why it really is that women on the whole don't lead and what it would actually take to increase the proportion of women leaders from 8 per cent worldwide to 52 per cent. I agreed that the shortage of women's leadership was, in part, due to the lack of money available to us for campaigns. But I also knew that, with all the money in the world, there would still be millions of women hesitating and holding back. Most women would refuse to run for office even if they were given all the funds they needed.

Also, running for office was not the only leadership activity women shied away from. Even the idea of chairing a local committee, or speaking in front of a crowd, or putting forward an idea in a departmental meeting, even just saying what they really think to a man in authority, can terrify some women into silence.

I began to speculate about what it would actually take to get women leading in proportion to our numbers, particularly if we were going to try to do it within thirty years. It did not seem to me to be as just simple as raising money. The stakes holding women down seemed to be deep inside of us, driven into our hearts and minds before we were even aware of politics, fund-raising or leadership of any kind.

Getting women into leadership in large enough numbers to make a difference would require us to keep up a regular daily onslaught against sexism, within a firm, reliable structure of encouragement. It would require us to excavate our real selves from the rubble of sexism – every day.

Thinking partnerships can do this.

I believe that the next step for women is to change not only the societal structures that disempower us, but the policies that fuel them, and most importantly the *thinking conditions* under which those policies are made. This book is intended to help us do that.

How far can we go? We can go as far as the barriers let us. Then we have to decide. We can stop. We can retreat. Or we can remove the barriers and proceed.

A WOMEN'S WORKSHOP FOR YOU

I encourage you to enjoy these pages as a kind of women's empowerment workshop. You are very, very welcome here.

Like the workshops, this book begins and ends with you. While reading it, give yourself time to be immersed in your own thoughts; consider for yourself without criticism or rush the things you really do want in your life and the possibilities for your leadership in the world. Give yourself time to look at the barriers that have held you hostage and to consider the opportunities to remove them.

This book is for all women. Every woman's empowerment is important. Thinking partnerships between women to remove the barriers to our power are effective across all identities. Whatever your background, class, race, nationality, or physical ability, age, sexual preference, religion or political perspective it is your full expression and positive impact on our world that this book addresses. Women can help each other because a thinking environment allows us to think *with* each other, not for each other; and to think *for* ourselves, not by ourselves. We understand each other because we are far more similar to one another than we are different.

The fact that you have picked up this book says something about you. It is an act of power for a woman just to consider empowerment. And it is a statement of the respect you have for yourself and for other women that you have chosen to explore this subject.

I begin the book with a description of a thinking environment, making a distinction between conditioning and thinking. I then look at ways sexism has disempowered women and dehumanized men, suggesting that women as a group are particularly well-trained to lead because our culture as women has encouraged us to produce a thinking environment. I have discussed three kinds of thinking required in leadership (structural, promotional and interactive) and shown that the experience of women, including the work of mothering, uses all three kinds of thinking.

I suggest what it will take for all women to see ourselves as leaders, to lead more humanly than our predecessors, and to break through the barriers to our power day after day.

The book tells you, step by step, how to establish a thinking partnership with another woman and how to use it to move forward in your life and leadership. It tells you how to turn your life and work into an environment where people can think, enjoy, create and change. It suggests that every issue of our time is ours to think about afresh and that, as experts in a thinking environment, we can begin to make this happen all around us.

This book is also a warm invitation to men who know they want change and know that what is truly good for women is also good for men. It is an invitation to join with women in the relief and fun of letting go of sexist conditioning and to create a positive partnership with women, a collaboration of equals to create thinking environments together and to generate ideas never before thought of about the issues we face and the world we want. Men and women have everything to gain from repudiating our sexist training and returning to our fully human, powerful, intelligent selves.

The people I have worked with have come from many groups, backgrounds and cultures. But I speak as myself, from my own experience – as a white, middle-class, heterosexual, able-bodied, forty-six-year-old, Southern United States, married, self-employed, England-residing, Quaker, red-headed, left-handed, female twin. I cannot speak as or for anyone else.

As you read this book, I hope you will consider speaking out for yourself, as yourself, about the issues of most importance to you, that you will speak publicly and privately, and that you will encourage others to do the same. There are innumerable stories and important new ideas waiting inside all of us. We need to treat each other to them.

Over the past twenty years I have found cause for hope. I have seen people help each other and begin to remove barriers in ways that take my breath away. I have watched people, thinking afresh together, begin to change systems they've lived with for years and find answers they'd never before imagined. I have seen new courage start to shine out from formerly wincing faces. I have seen women step forward in the world who had never before ventured past the safety of saying 'maybe later.'

When you have an effect on even one other person, you are leading. You can start now to make that sphere of influence a thinking environment and to enlarge it step by step.

If we throw away our assumptions, remove the barriers, and begin truly to think for ourselves, 'Women and power – how far can we go?' becomes a very interesting question.

A Note on Usage

One of my favourite interests is linguistics. At university I enjoyed more than anything else the hours I spent literally sitting in the *Oxford English Dictionary* – it was in twenty volumes, each two feet tall. In fact I soon became a word-usage fanatic.

But about twenty years ago I had to recognize the fact that words evoke images in the human mind and those images control our attitudes and our behaviour. Images can promote or hold back whole groups of people. And no matter how energetically we in my field of English insist that some words *can* mean two opposite things at once, I eventually had to admit that this theory was not workable in practice. In particular the word 'he' cannot, in the imagery of the mind, mean 'she'.

So I, like thousands of others, spent the 1970s searching for a neuter substitute. I found, though, that I could not bear the awkwardness of saying 'he/she' and 'his/her', nor the objectification of saying 'its', nor the revenge tactic of using 'she' to mean both genders. But one day I discovered that in Anglo-Saxon, a respectable ancestor of modern English, 'they' and 'their' were used in the singular, as well as the plural, to designate either male or female.

So for years now, relieved by this link with antiquity, I have been using 'they' and 'their' to mean 'his' or 'her', 'he' or 'she'. If you find that this practice still jars, consider the discomfort a price worth paying in order to end the systematic exclusion of women from centres of power. Or perhaps remind yourself that so-called 'pure' and 'correct' language is probably one of the most unstable elements in our lives. Much of what we now call 'correct usage' is in fact a 'corruption' of earlier 'purer' English which was in turn a 'corruption' of forms before it. Language purity is really a naive, falacious, racist, classist concept we should just toss away. It is much more fun, as well as less bigoted, to swim with the language changes instead of damming the shore. The tide breaks through eventually anyway.

I must admit, though, I still have trouble with 'vision' as a verb. I simply cannot 'vision' something, or 'action' it. I hate the way it 'impacts' on my life. I suppose I find it easier to enjoy linguistic change when it offers hope of restoring power and dignity to a group of human beings. My studies of English would have been even more interesting if they had been placed in that context. 'English Grammar as a Tool for Liberation': I would have signed up for that course even if the lectures had been at 8 am on a Saturday.

PART 1

The Thinking Environment in Theory

I believe that women will move rapidly into power, changing for the better the way people lead, just as soon as we understand why our experience as women has prepared us beautifully for leadership I also believe that men will happily change the way they lead once they see that women's culture offers an end to the brutality they have experienced as men.

This section of the book explores how women and men, because of our gender, have been treated and how that treatment has shaped our thinking, our leadership, and our world. I encourage you to imagine the changes we could make if women and men could claim the strengths and avoid the dangers of both our gender cultures. Women and men are natural partners in power: we need the information in this book to ensure that we build that partnership successfully.

CHAPTER 1

Why Women Must Lead

As a woman you have been trained for leadership since birth. You have been taught the values that leadership should embody. You have been encouraged to use skills that leadership at its best employs. And you have learned these things. You have practised and practised. You know them deep in your bones.

But no one has called them leadership. In fact, most likely, you have become convinced that these things you have learned are not important. They are just the everyday experience of 'being a woman'. The world has always depended on this leadership from you, and time and time again you have delivered. But too often you have done this amazing job as a buttress to others' leadership. You have done it as the strong underpinning, the point of stability, the quiet core of what works.

And yet, if we were to take a close look at what girlhood and womanhood teach us, I think we would find that what is needed most of all in today's public leadership is the very ability women have been encouraged to develop in private – the ability to think interactively and, in so doing, to create a *thinking environment*.

I believe that creating a thinking environment, the set of conditions under which human beings can think best, is one of humanity's most important leadership tasks. Without it we do stupid things, irreversibly deadly things. Without it, leaders control rather than create, they conquer rather than empower, they incarcerate rather than encourage. Without a thinking environment, we eventually destroy each other.

With it, we thrive.

There may be nothing more important than this. And yet the world's devaluing of everything in 'women's sphere' means that we do not see these interactive skills as leadership skills, nor do we usually see ourselves as leaders. This constant, underlying devaluation of women is one of the biggest internal barriers between us and our power.

The key skill in creating a thinking environment is interactive thinking, a skill women are encouraged to develop and men are steered away from. Women are taught from their earliest years that their excellence *as women* will be judged by the way they *interact with* people and by whether or not people flourish in their care. Men are taught that their excellence *as men* will be judged by the way they *control* people, by how well they promote themselves, and by whether or not they stay 'on top'.

Male conditioning steers men away from interactive thinking. Men's conditioning encourages them to think in terms of win or lose, all or nothing, us or them. It puts great emphasis on being right, on getting credit, on being 'objective', on argument and debate. It also encourages sidestepping, deflecting attention from the real issues, and skimming the surface. Men are encouraged to be good at interactive thinking in relation to things (when inventing new products and systems, for example) but not in relation to people. Women, on the other hand, are encouraged to think interactively with and about people from the minute we are born.

These two messages create very different cultures and approaches to problems; they also create very different kinds of leaders. Controlling leaders keep people from thinking; their purpose is to herd others. Interactive leaders ignite people's thinking; their purpose is to launch others.

Women's ability to create a thinking environment and to think interactively is encouraged but not valued. It is not even seen as a set of skills. It does not appear on resumés. It is certainly never described as leadership. If talked about at all, it is dismissed as haphazard, unscientific, soft and dispensable. And yet, ironically, on those occasions when men's leadership results in a truly human outcome, it is primarily these 'soft, dispensable', flexible aspects of their behaviour, untouched by male conditioning, that have produced the fine achievement. The world applauds men's heavy hand. But it is men's suppleness that triumphs.

As women we have been encouraged to create and sustain life. Even when we have been bitter victims, we have generally groped for the most human outcome. In our families, in our relationships, in our offices and in our communities, religious groups, and marketplaces we have learned how to treat people well, we have supported their growth, and we have recognized the importance of unleashing their best thinking. As women we have not been conditioned to extinguish; we have been encouraged to create. We have not been conditioned to think *for* people; we have been taught how to think *with* them. Now we need to understand that, in doing this, we have been leading.

Creating a thinking environment is an intrinsically human ability, not a gender trait. But women have traditionally been rewarded for this behaviour and are taught to see it as particularly womanly. Men, on the other hand, have been taught that real men don't waste their time that way. Women, as a result, more readily retain these interactive thinking environment skills. Men, as a group, tend to suppress them.

Women's culture – the set of general attitudes, approaches and behaviour that females (of whatever other multiplicity of cultures we represent) are encouraged to develop *because we are female* – is a sensible, intelligent, interactive, aware and caring culture. It is inside the gender cultures that men and women learn the most indelible lessons of how to live. Women's culture, at its best, teaches us to notice, to think incisively, to put human needs first, to draw people towards their best, and to value closeness. At its worst, our culture tells us to put each other and ourselves last (if anywhere at all), and to look to men as our authorities and for our significance.

Men's culture, on the other hand, requires men *as men* to hurt each other, to dominate, to trap people, to ridicule, to control. Inside this conditioning men, *as men*, cannot afford to support people in thinking afresh and for themselves. As men they must prove their own worth by being better than others, by making others look stupid or incompetent. Men's culture – that set of beliefs, attitudes and behaviour that men must develop in order to be considered *real men* – is a disconnected, violent, demeaning, controlling culture. Inside it, men learn to lead by disempowering others, to win by defeating others, to 'think' by arguing with others, to enforce change by silencing others. At a young age they grow distrustful of each other and sometimes unable to remember what real closeness is.

And, yes, there are women who hurt people, women who do not help people to think afresh or for themselves, and who are a central impediment in people's lives and development. Individually women can behave badly, and individually women can and have put a stop to people's thinking.

But we are not, *as women*, required to do this. Our identity *as women*, our most fundamental sense of who we are, is not threatened by our helping others to think and to achieve. We do not prove ourselves to be *real women* by holding in check the power of other people. Women do not define themselves as a group by rolling over the lives of others.

Women's individual pathologies can lead us to inflict pain on others. We can react to our collective oppression by becoming manipulative, deceitful, seducible and furious. And our emulation of male-conditioned behaviour can make us espouse the shortsighted and inhuman ideas that male conditioning generates. (Too often by the time women reach the senior management level of male-run organizations, their values have been co-opted in exactly this way.) But this behaviour is not an attempt to prove ourselves to be real women. Women's culture is not a brutal culture.

THE INVITATION TO WOMEN

In many parts of the world there are new initiatives to increase women's opportunities to lead. As we touch the tip of the year 2000, big companies, the military, the scientific and legal professions and government are making renewed commitments to recruit women. This is a welcome form of progress. To have been systematically excluded from these jobs has been flagrant sexism. And these places of work need women more than they realize.

Yet there is danger lurking just beneath the sugar-coated surface of some of these invitations. And if we can recognize it, we can outsmart it. The danger lies in the fact that we are not only being invited into new roles as leaders of these companies and organizations. We are also being lured into the leadership halls of male conditioning and culture.

The invitation includes the message that it is the way men, locked inside male conditioning, have run the world that we must copy if we want to be accomplished and powerful. Like men, we are being offered the chance to confine ourselves, disconnect from our hearts, compete, narrow our vision, limit our thinking, and even destroy. That is what men, through their conditioning, have been forced to do in professional work, economics, and medicine, law, government, science, religion, business, and most unequivocally in the military.

In the midst of this widely publicized support for women's leadership development, men do not seem to be coming to us and saying, 'We want to join you and be led by you, to learn more about women's culture so that our companies and systems can serve humanity more effectively. We need your leadership because you still possess some of the facets of human thinking that our conditioning has forced many of us to lay aside. Join us at the top and show us what to do.'

Instead men, controlled by their culture, are saying to us, 'Right, a few more of you can join us here. But you will have to act like us. Leave your experience as women – as mothers, as sisters and lovers, as nurses and volunteers and community organizers and artists – at the door. Come in if you have the stamina for it. We will test you, more severely than we test each other, and if you pass, you can have a bit more control – for as long as we say.'

Men once again are becoming the architects of our liberation.

The sad thing to watch, as we begin another era of women's advancement, is the way we jump at the invitation. We don't see or value our experience as women. We've been made to think that men achieve the most important things and that the way they do things is the best way to do them. Invited into their seats of power, we agree largely to leave behind and devalue our women's culture and to bludgeon ourselves with the messages men have endured.

We respond with, 'Thank you, I accept, and I agree to put all my energies into being aggressive [and call it being assertive], into doing down the 'competitor' [and call it enterprise], into lying [and call it diplomacy], into obsession [and call it loyalty], into exploitation [and call it resourcefulness], into conquest [and call it victory], into addiction [and call it reward], and into control [and call it power]. I will not cry or demand patience or expect tenderness. I will not help my competitors. I will not be wrong. I will be grateful to you for this opportunity to abandon myself. And I will encourage other women to do the same.'

We must beware.

We must decline this part of the invitation. It is not women's advancement. It is dangerous seduction.

As we participate in these good initiatives we will find many women eager to step forward and lead. But we will find, too, that an alarming number of women will not choose to take advantage of new leadership.

Many will be too unsure of themselves, many will not want to risk advancement for fear of eclipsing the men in their lives; and many will say as Jackie, a young woman considering leadership in her school, said to her best friend, 'If I have to start competing with you and lose you in order to lead, I'm not interested. And if I have to act as if I have no feelings, I'm not interested.' She was thirteen then. Today she is just setting out on her adult career path. We will have to launch initiatives that encourage the millions of women who hold back in this way to see themselves as leaders and to realize that they can redesign leadership to be compatible with their values.

Historically women have sought work where the humanity is, not where the brutality is. Many women, in medicine, for example, have chosen paediatrics, the education for which is more humane than that of surgery. Women in economics have chosen retail sales where human interactions are more important than in stockbroking or arranging takeover bids. But we must now encourage each other to enter all fields of work and in doing so to change them, bringing our human values to them. We must no longer hide in what is comfortable, but we must also resist being brutalized. We must do things the way women would do them if we were giving no thought to what men think.

Women will grasp these opportunities if they can be trained to trust their own thinking, to value their culture as women and to change the corridors of power as they walk them. Those women who are currently involved in expanding women's leadership opportunities can best serve other women by assisting them to stay true to their real selves and lead from there.

We can also seek out the men who will happily join us and even encourage us to move further in this direction. I often think of the early morning a few years ago when Christopher, now my husband, and I were climbing a hill at Sharrow Bay in the Lake District. I had stopped, frightened of the steeper slopes ahead and had turned to gaze at the beauty that stretched out below me. I called to him to say how lovely it was. The water and fields beyond shimmered. But he had climbed on ahead, beyond my fear. And from many metres up I heard him say, 'It's lovely where you are. But look from here.' I weighed it carefully – my pleasure, my fear, and the possibilities I couldn't yet see. Eventually, I turned, looked up, and climbed the distance.

We will find answers to the questions facing our world by thinking from inside the best of male and female cultures and from outside the worst of them. The answers will come from a strong thinking environment. We are not, for example, going to solve the problems of homelessness just by building more shelters, or of mothers just by giving tax relief for child care, or of leadership just with more access to the boardroom, or of crumbling Communist regimes simply with currently practised market-driven economics. We have got to go far, far beyond our obsession with making rigid systems work. They never will. And we will deplete ourselves in the process of trying.

Instead, we must leave our desks and work benches and podiums and committee rooms and Hoovers and assembly lines and microscopes for enough time every day *to meet together and think*. We must start afresh, clear the slate of assumptions and traditions, and ask ourselves until we can formulate good answers, 'What do I really think?' and 'What do I, free of rigid gender conditioning, really want?' and 'What will actually be best for all people?'

We have the minds to leap out of the frames of reference that control our organizations, our institutions and our relationships and, having taken that leap, we can start imagining the wild, wonderful and infinitely sensible things that will finally solve our problems and structure our world the way we've always wanted it structured.

To do this we must learn how to meet together and how to treat each other so well that our thinking reaches a new level. And then we must support each other in ways that will encourage each of us to do something decisive with those ideas.

It is time now for women to look at the things we do when we are being ourselves, when we are not looking over our shoulders at how men think things should be done. We need to see how intelligent we are, and in particular how well we think about human situations and about our planet. We need to see that our women's culture has taught us how to think and hold on to our humanity at the same time. It has taught us to stay connected to ourselves and to other people while we think about difficult issues. As we start to populate formerly male-dominated fields, we have the opportunity to change them.

Tamsin, a scientist colleague of mine, recently asked me how I thought she could ever convince the leaders in her company to learn and practise the skills of a thinking environment. 'Too much of the time the male managers here won't consider change and are defensive, even punitive, when I suggest improvements and new directions. I am getting terribly discouraged and even scared. I am afraid it is going to take years to get them to come around to wanting a thinking environment.'

Many, many women feel this kind of discouragement. It is a product of another kind of sexism at work – women assuming that the world will be changed by men and that our contribution will be to change the men who change the world.

Women can change the world. We do not have to change men first. We only have to lead them back into our culture. Men will change when they live inside women's culture long enough to rediscover the interactive selves they lost as a result of male conditioning. Women will soon see their own culture clearly and confidently enough to know how to invite men in. Men's groups, men's awareness meetings and creative thinking management courses can sometimes help. But they are not enough on their own to do the job of restoring men to their interactively fluent selves. Men will have to live inside women's culture in order to achieve this.

Men will also change when they decide to ask women what men can do to ensure that women become 52 per cent of the leadership of the world – and then do it. Good things will happen for men if they can do this. Even their toughest military decisions, however, have not required this level of courage and determination. Fortunately, men have the mettle for it. Hearteningly, some men have already begun.

'Look at it another way,' I said to Tamsin. 'If women will change the world, men will eventually follow us.'

To achieve this, we will need to refine and practise our interactive thinking skills; take leadership positions now at whatever level we can, advancing step by step; and turn all our spheres of influence into thinking environments. Soon men will show interest. They will see the benefits and want to learn from us. As women go forward, men over time will follow.

Sometimes, however, the best way to get someone to go with you is simply to go.

CHAPTER 2

The Thinking Environment

When something is not valued, it is invisible. An object, an idea or a personal quality can be right in front of us, but because we do not value it, we look past it. This is true of women's thinking environment abilities. We have them in abundamce. We use them every day. They are right in front of us. But because they are not valued, we hardly recognize them.

What is it women do when we are at our best together? What exactly is this support we give each other? What is the special way we relate to each other when there are no men around? At our best, how do we help each other think, so casually and so well? We cannot exactly say. We just do it. But if these thinking environment skills are the most important qualifcations of a leader, as I have suggested, then we need to demystify this behaviour and name the skills clearly. We need to pull into conscious view the abilities we use intuitively, so that we can refine them, teach them and make them the conscious centrepiece of our leadership.

A thinking environment is the set of conditions under which people think best. It is the circumstance in which good solutions are found, good policies are made, and in which we can remove the barriers to our power. A thinking environment is a time between two human beings in which both are able to think with uninhibited creativity, incisiveness and pleasure. But it is even more wonderful than that. A thinking environment, because it produces the best possible relationships between people, is one of the things we want most in our lives.

We all long for a thinking environment. We fantasize about it. We look for it in almost every interaction. When our eyes meet someone else's eyes and we make even the most laconic connection, something in us stirs; in the hope that that person will be genuinely interested in us, will take us on our own terms, will respect us, and will want to know what we really think. Our hope, however submerged in shyness or busyness, is that now, uninterrupted and unjudged, we may be able to sort out our thoughts and feelings and move forward in our life. And, reciprocally, we hope that the other person will disclose equally genuine thoughts of their own, trusting us to help them as well.

In a thinking environment one person takes a genuine interest in the other's ideas. Their attention is on the development of that person's thoughts and feelings, on unravelling them thoroughly, on resolving the inconsistencies between them, on removing the assumptions that halt the next thought, on unearthing one idea after another, until the person reaches a new understanding. Neither person is focused on being 'right'. And neither has an emotional or political investment in the outcome of the exchange. Their only concern is that the best possible idea should emerge and that each person should think as clearly and independently as possible.

Unfortunately, thinking itself has gained a bad reputation. Because it is commonly used to mean cognitive and analytical activity only, it has become associated with a disembodied process having very little to do with real life, feelings, hard work or true love. It is seen as the reserve of a few white, boring men who have no effect on the real world and who can't be bothered to talk to the rest of us. It is supposed to have had its origins in ancient Greece (as if the ancient Eastern world never existed) and to continue behind the slide rules (remember those?) of pudgy boys. It is maligned as tedious and unthrilling.

Ironically, it is also seen as highly evolved, the thing that distinguishes humans from other animals, and the intellectual élite from the rest of us. In fact, most of the oppressive messages about marginalized groups in our society centre on thinking: if we are women, we can't think because we are too emotional; if we are working class, we can't think because we just do what we are told; if we are Irish or Welsh or Scottish or Polish, we can't think because we are not English; if we are from the North of England, we can't think because we are not from the South; if we are African or Arab or Native American or Aboriginal Australian or Chinese or Japanese or Korean or Indian or Latin

American, we can't think because we are not white; if we are young, we can't think because we haven't lived long enough; if we are old, we can't think because we have lived too long; if we are lesbians or gay men, we can't think because there is something wrong with us; if we are artists, we can't think because we can only intuit.

But none of these statements is true. Thinking belongs to all of us. And often it is thrilling.

I use the word *thinking* to describe the vast, multi-faceted process of intelligence that includes feelings, creativity, speculation and intuition as well as cognition, analysis and computation. Thinking in this context is the *full* use of the human mind and heart.

A thinking environment is the behaviour and circumstance that allow the mind to work at its best. Creating it requires people to do only ten basic things with each other. Although these ten components of a thinking environment are rare in our lives, they are not difficult to assemble. They require no elaborate resources: no PhD, no special equipment, no gimmicks and no expense account. They are rare only because we have not insisted that the people around us understand and use them. I encourage you, wherever you have influence, to reinstate these components in individual interactions and in groups.

THE TEN COMPONENTS OF A THINKING ENVIRONMENT – A BRIEF LOOK

LISTENING

Listening is much more than a matter of not talking. It is also an act of genuine interest in what the person is saying and in their thinking process. When you listen, you have to turn all your attention to the thinker. You also have to want to help that person come up with *their* finest thinking.

In a thinking environment you listen, not in order to find the flaws in your partner's thinking with which you can debate and humiliate the person, but in order to get the scope of the issues the person is addressing, notice where the person's thinking is stuck and help to remove the barriers that are in their way. You are with the person to enjoy their mind at work and to be midwife to a brand-new good idea, not in order to seem brilliant or to get your own way. For many people, this is hard because we are trained to prove ourselves by being the one with the good ideas, not by helping someone else to find them.

My friend Sally summed it up well when she said, 'I want you to consult me and then I want you to wait; to wait and wait and wait, until I can answer. I don't want you to answer for me.'

It is often said that you cannot talk about an issue until you understand it. I think it is more likely that you cannot understand an issue until you can talk about it. Listening to each other is this important.

INCISIVE QUESTIONS

Asking incisive questions is probably the most powerful component of a thinking environment. An incisive question is one that removes the barriers in a person's thinking.

'If' questions are particularly useful because they take the barrier away directly: 'If you were not afraid, what would you do?' for example, or 'If this situation could be made exactly right for you, how would it look?' Any question that plucks out the barriers – fear and obligation in these two cases – is incisive.

Two other excellent incisive questions are: 'What do you really want?' and 'What do you really think?' But the most incisive question is always the one that is tailored precisely for the person you are listening to at that moment. If the question sweeps away useless assumptions and frees us to generate ideas we had no access to before, it is incisive.

Incisive questions never humiliate. They are kind. They are clear. They allow the person to speak honestly. In their presence thinking resumes.

APPRECIATION: THE TEN TO ONE RATIO

We think best when we are appreciated. Our doubts and self-flagellations only distract us. So we must give up the tedious habit of demeaning ourselves.

There is a taboo against self-appreciation – it is widely considered to be unnecessary, unholy, unprofessional and un-English. This is a pity, because one of the most effective ways to bring a person back to the pulse of their own ideas is an accurate word of appreciation.

In fact, I find that the environment needs to be about *ten times more appreciative* than it is critical for the highest level of clear new thinking to take place. (If a ten to one ratio seems impossible to you, reaching for it may mean that you achieve at least two to one – and that would be an improvement.) Generally, unfortunately, our relationships and places of work are the reverse: people in an ordinary day encounter about ten times more criticism than appreciation, which may in part account for the generally mediocre thinking dominating our world.

People argue that this change in the ratio of appreciation to criticism will lower standards and keep people from correcting mistakes. Not so. People more readily notice and correct their mistakes when the balance is tipped decisively in favour of appreciation.

When leaders, managers, parents and teachers have changed just this one element in their interactions with people, they have found a surprising increase in the level of well-grounded, original thinking around them.

ENCOURAGEMENT

When we are stuck, when our brains produce only the old, never-did-work-anyway ideas, we need another person's belief in us. We need it explicitly. It won't do for our colleagues just to *assume* that we know we can do it. Instead, they can remind us in all sorts of ways that we *can* think and that we can find a solution that will work well for everyone.

Staggering numbers of people reach adulthood with their heads bowed and their initiative spent, deeply and chronically discouraged. It is no wonder that generation after generation the same small number of people invent, inspire and lead. It is no wonder that the same old ideas replace the same old ideas in cycles of unworkability. We need to replace 'It will never work' with 'You can do it.' The results of this change will belie its simplicity.

EQUALITY

We think best with peers. There is something about holding each other in mutual respect that keeps our minds purring. Conversely, to feel 'inferior to' someone or 'better than' someone can keep our minds from venturing out into new, creative territory. If we already feel lacking, we will, in the presence of 'higher rank', feel even more so and we will hardly be able to think at all. If we are in the presence of 'lower rank', believing that the other person cannot operate at our 'higher' level, we will not bother to solicit good ideas from them. Nor will we allow them to help us think and – surprise, surprise – they won't. Judging each other in this way aborts hundreds of good ideas.

It doesn't matter who we are, where we live, where we went to school, what family we grew up in, how much money we make, or how thick or thin our résumés are, we are potentially thinking giants. We must treat each other this way.

DIVERSITY

Human beings *think* better in diversity than we do in homogeneity. This seems to have something to do with our need for reality. What is real acts as a catalyst to thinking. What is not real – including sameness, patronizing attitudes, tokenism and colour-blindness – acts as a control.

So, a group of all-white fifty-year-old males think less well together than a mix of men, women, black, white, gay, wheelchair-bound, deaf, young and old people. This is partly because a diverse group inevitably draws on a wider range of experience, but also because in the presence of diversity the mind stretches and yawns, finds balance and dares to move.

The key to making diversity work is pride. Participants in a thinking environment have to like who they are, they have to 'come to the table' *as themselves* and draw on what they know to be true from their real experience. If they are ashamed of the many groups they come from, they will try to blend into the dominant group, and nothing interesting will happen. On the other hand, if they think and speak proudly *as themselves*, they will think and speak with greater range, depth, freshness and insight.

BOUNDARIES

You are thinking about an issue. You have sorted through the ways people have always done this thing. The possibility of a new idea is occurring to you. Then the person listening to you kisses you on the mouth.

Or you find, at last, the key solution to a problem, the one that will also solve the other problems you are dealing with. Slowly but bravely you consider that solution. Then your partner's brow furrows.

Or you have begun to sweep away a formerly rock-hard assumption in your thinking: you have decided not to let lack of capital stop you from pursuing your goal. Now money is not a factor, new and better ideas start to unfold. You are thrilled. Then your partner offers you a loan.

Keeping the boundaries clear and sacred between thinking partners is essential for thinking to progress. A thinking environment, while simple, is nevertheless delicate. Like most natural structures, it can collapse when its boundaries are invaded. Thinking works best when there is room to move around, free from the danger of running into the other person's needs.

FEELINGS

'I have just spent £4000 and two years finding out that feelings are all right and now you want me to *think* again!' This workshop participant was trapped in the assumption that when human beings think, they stop feeling. No. In fact, the more alienated we are from our feelings, the drier and more repetitive our thinking becomes. Afraid of feelings, we spend too much of our thinking time strategizing unconsciously how to avoid them. We think instead of feel and that can be dangerous.

The thinking partner must remain at ease when strong feelings surface in the thinker. A thinking environment recognizes that thinking and feeling are a beautifully intertwined mechanism in the human being. When one takes place, the other is likely to happen too. Releasing our feelings (by crying or laughing, for example) helps us to think more clearly, and thinking clearly helps us to feel more deeply.

The listener, however, must make sure that she is not imposing *her* own feelings on the thinker. As a thinking partner she maintains a dispassionate attitude towards the thinker, an attitude of interest but with no emotional investment in the outcome. She needs to be emotionally invested in the opportunity for the *best* idea to emerge, not for *her* idea to emerge.

PHYSICAL ENVIRONMENT
· ·

A thinking environment is not just intellectual; it is also physical. When it is right, it is comfortable for everyone. It is also attractive, clean, warm, safe, light and physically accessible to people of any sort of physical ability or challenge. The environment should, by its beauty, its clarity, its warmth and its accessibility welcome you, confirm that you are good, intelligent and valuable. It should say clearly that it recognizes and honours your physical needs. It can then better keep your spirits lifted and your attention on the thinking in progress, not on the environment itself.

The inside of the human body must also be a thinking environment. It, too, must be as well cared for and respected as possible. We think best when our attention is not drawn to our bodies. Keeping your body cherished, fit and addiction-free is part of creating a thinking environment.

INFORMATION
· ·

We can think well about an issue to the extent that we have correct information about it. Some issues lend themselves more easily to this information-gathering process than do others. If the issue is financial, we can get the figures. If it is sociological, we can get the statistics. If it is medical, we can get the test results.

But if it is the formulation of a new policy affecting people's lives, we must probe in all sorts of places to become well enough informed. This is a big job. It requires us to find out about people's *actual life* experience. We need to find out by living in their situation somehow, or by at least asking about their lives directly. We need to find out all we can know that we can never really know, and keep asking and listening.

The ten components of a thinking environment are rare because they are not reinforced either in social training or at school. In fact, they are specifically undermined. From childhood onwards we continually hear messages like: don't ask too many questions; don't look at a person too long; don't compliment people – they will think you want something; crying gets you nowhere; some people are naturally better than others; you can't trust people who are different from you; helping people means solving their problems for them; there are some things that are just not possible; know your place; don't probe; a messy desk is the sign of a creative mind; spare the rod and spoil the child; trust the experts; don't question authority; success comes from defeating your opponents – if you have silenced them, you have won.

There is also a strong gender-related reason behind the scarcity of a thinking environment: females are encouraged to develop the ten skills but are told by the male-dominated world that these skills are not valuable, and males are not encouraged to develop these skills because they are too 'womanly' for tough-guy conditioning to stand.

And so, though we may long for a thinking environment in our lives and work, and though the world desperately needs a thinking environment everywhere, we have little chance of achieving it until we understand its skills, refine them, acknowledge their value, and then teach them to our friends and colleagues. They are usually happy to be taught. Like us, they already know these skills unconsciously. All we need is permission to use them.

Creating a thinking environment is not a mountainous task. One component feeds naturally into the next and eventually an environment is created. Soon the hard questions, like the ones about the barriers to our power, ease into answers; and over time our lives change.

CHAPTER 3

Sexism as a Thinking Barrier

For as long as I can remember I have wondered why human beings can be intelligent one minute and rigid the next. When I was five, I asked my mother why my friend Brian had such great ideas when we played cowboys and cowgirls in the back garden but laughed at me when I asked him over to play dolls. Mother liked my asking questions. But this one made her quiet. I think she preferred the ones about what made water go down the plughole a certain way. Gravity was somehow easier to explain than sexism.

We may never really know why human thinking goes rigid, what goes on in the brain that makes us conceive of and then do things that are dull, illogical or hurtful, sometimes over and over again. Much has been written on the subject of human intelligence but most of it, however widely accepted, is still speculation. The brain is a vast and mighty work of art.

What we do know is that it is not possible to isolate the human mind, to carve it out of its surroundings, spread it under a microscope and objectively observe what it does, free of any external influences. From the time the brain first starts to exist in a human foetus it is already in an intensely complex environment of human feelings, physical stimulation and repeated experience. Asking whether the thinking that precedes behaviour is induced genetically or environmentally (the nature versus nurture debate) is essentially a waste of time because, regardless of the age of the research subject, scientists can never take the brain out of the environment nor the environment out of the brain.

What we can do, however, is work with people to help them restore the clarity and originality of their thinking. If we could remove even 50 per cent of these environmental factors, and prevent their further spread in our children, we might begin to see an end to the poverty of society's thinking.

Women could then begin to live with fewer barriers to our power. The internal barriers that make us turn back just as we have begun the climb out of our limits as women, that make us sneer at each other's advances instead of pursuing our own, that make us quiet and then bitter, that let men decide what happens to us, that keep us complacent about making up less than 10 per cent of the leadership of the world – all these come from rigidities in our thinking. Our actions are determined by our thinking. So it is at the level of *thinking*, not just action, that we must address the issue of women's power.

Some of these thinking rigidities are caused by individual experiences inflicted on us in childhood. One person's perceptions will be uniquely rigid, and unlike the rigid perceptions of another person. For example, I may refuse to take out the rubbish because a neighbour chased me round the block with a garter snake when I was six and threw it and me into a rubbish bin, whereas you may be happy to take the rubbish out, but be unable to complete a sentence when church bells are ringing because as a child you were beaten for crying on your way to church.

Another type of rigidity in human thinking affects groups of people. Racism, sexism, ageism, anti-semitism and homophopia are some of the many forms it takes. Group rigidities are introduced into the brain just as painfully as individual rigidities, but their messages vary little from person to person. One racist person thinks similarly to another racist person. In fact, whole countries can carry the same rigid ideas about whole other countries. This is known as cultural conditioning.

Cultural conditioning is any immobile attitude towards groups of people which has been instilled into our minds without our knowing it, and then reinforced by repetition and physical or emotional pain. It lives as an undifferentiated, semi-gelatinous blob in our minds. Making no distinction between one situation and another, it tells us how to see people and how to treat them at all times. These attitudes are ground in so repetitively and steadily from childhood that they warp our sophis-ticated thinking mechanisms and make them misfire. The ideas that come from them are twisted, irrelevant and harmful.

We permit cultural conditioning to pitch camp in our brains because its perpetrators threaten us with ridicule, ostracism, more pain and even death if we do not. Its perpetrators are usually big – adults, schools, governments, armies, television. And, at the time when we are most vulnerable to them, we are usually little. This process can make us act like bullies, feel like victims, and conceive of ideas that attack rather than solve.

Conditioning begins with false assumptions and draws faulty conclusions. It masquerades as thinking. But it is not the same as thinking.

Very few people operate within cultural conditioning all the time. Most people continually weave (not to say careen) between real thinking and conditioning. Even on a given topic a person can think clearly and independently one moment and as a pawn the next.

I believe that with the right tools and enough work we can recover our thinking flexibility. Some of the best tools for this are the ten components of a thinking environment. Drop a conditioned attitude into a thinking environment and you will see it splinter and crack in the face of careful attention and incisive questions from the listener. Conditioning just can't hold together in a thinking environment. Everything about the environment runs counter to the conditioning, challenging it, loosening the emotional mortar that held it in place, and in a surprisingly short time, freeing the mind to return to generating ideas of integrity.

SEXISM AND HUMAN NATURE

Of the many stupidities of cultural conditioning that beset the circuitry of our minds, one of the most dangerous is sexism. Sexism asks us to believe that men are better than women.

I believe that women and men are by nature equally human, equally intelligent, equally incisive, equally caring and courageous. Both genders can think, love, muse, leap, wait, imagine, calculate, co-operate, command and care. Nature did not place one gender on a pedestal and one at the helm, nor intend one of us to create the mess and one to clean it up, nor one of us to nurture and the other to discipline. Both of us can lead and both of us can defer. Neither our biceps nor our breasts, nor our ovaries nor our testicles determine the degree of our toughness or tenderness. We can both be trained to be vicious. And treated well, we can both be counted on to be kind.

But sexism is not the same as human nature. Sexism is a brain parasite, a dangerous visitor who has to be asked to leave. Sexism is as rampant as ever in our lives, but it is fiercely denied. Some men have colonized this knowledge of sexism ('Oh, that's no longer a problem in this company; we have a woman on our board now') and some women have apologized for it ('I'm not a feminist but . . '). Some young men have shrugged it off ('If she wants to protect herself let her buy the condoms') and young women have ridden past it ('It's really not the problem it was in my mother's generation').

The danger here is not just that sexism still exists, but that our society is tired of talking about it. Females who bring up the subject of sexism are derided as 'feminists' (which is like deriding someone for being a human being), and males who talk about it are derided as 'disruptive'. As we grow tired of the subject, we give in to it. If we don't keep talking about it openly and graphically, our real selves will again retreat. And, not coincidentally, as women hide, species vanish, ozone goes, oil and coal diminish, the rainforests fail, half of Africa dies of AIDS, fields and pastures smother under instant housing developments that peel to ghettoes in two generations, incomes plummet, and tissue regresses into tumour.

We must face sexism. Minute by minute we must all look at what is right in front of us. We must unflaggingly refuse to deny that we live with sexism. We eat it and sleep with it and run our offices with it and raise our children by it. We read it on virtually every page of our newspapers, watch it on almost every popular TV programme, and see it in every Haagen Dazs and Calvin Klein Obsession ad. We work to exhaustion to get the money to buy it. We allow our loved ones to inject it into our brains and then we share the needles.

Facing it starts with talking about it. And talking about it is, fortunately, not nearly as draining as denying it. Instead of asking ourselves 'Is there any sexism here?' we can start with the question, 'What is the sexism here?' Then we can quickly ask with optimism, 'Now, what will we do about it?'

SEXIST CONDITIONING
AND LEADERSHIP THINKING
. . . .

Thinking takes many forms. Three forms of thinking necessary for good leadership are interactive, structural and promotional. Sexism has an effect on all three.

PROMOTIONAL THINKING

People use promotional thinking to present themselves and their ideas to the public. People who do this well have confidence in the value of their ideas, they expect to be well-received, and they are convinced that asserting themselves like this is preferable to being quiet. Promotional thinking is essential for widespread communication and change. Culturally men are strongly encouraged to go out into the world and think promotionally. Women are not.

I don't do this well.

STRUCTURAL THINKING

People use structural thinking to organize things, categorize things, compute, compare, contrast, or group things. Structural thinking enables us to find order in chaos, to rank things, to evaluate statistically and describe things, to create systems and themes, to define catchment areas and to make schedules agendae. Structural thinking is essential for us to see meaning in our world and to delineate a beginning, middle and end to our activities. The stereotype portrays men as good at structural thinking and women as bad at it. But in fact, culturally both women and men are encouraged to think structurally.

I do this well

INTERACTIVE THINKING

People think interactively when their minds move between and among disparate elements in order to create something new.

Virtually all human relations require interactive thinking. When people devise ways to relate to each other, when they inspire, when they co-operate, when they solve problems, when they reach a deep mutual understanding, they have had to bring together their own ideas or viewpoints with those of others and encourage the new thing born from the combination. This level of human interaction requires a particular awareness, patience, ability and integrity of thought. It also requires a particular kind of emotional connection with, openness to, and respectful interest and trust in the other person.

Interactive thinking requires people to:

1 Bring disparate things together to create a new idea.

2   Keep the whole picture in mind while focusing on the detail.

3   Assess ideas on their worth, not on their source.

4   Manage ambiguity, seeing several conflicting truths at once.

5   Remove thinking barriers, seeing new possibilities with every situation.

6   Have no personal emotional investment in the outcome of a person's thinking.

7   See issues from many perspectives, changing the frame of reference easily.

8   Identify the key issue which influences everything else.

9   Elicit people's real experiences, breaking through denial and ignorance.

10 Find the big issues below the surface, knowing that where there is a tip, there is an iceberg.

All thinking about human issues requires interactive thinking skills. Interactive thinking keeps things developing and changing and resolving. Women's culture encourages this skill; men's does not. It is inside this women's culture, as girls, quite unconscious that it is happening, that we develop these interactive thinking skills.

And yet these three kinds of thinking are not inherently gender related. Men and women use them equally well in places where sexist conditioning has not taken root. Because leadership requires all three kinds of thinking, we need both genders to operate competently in all three modes.

There are many ways to do this, and perhaps the most effective is to create a thinking environment wherever we are. The ten components help immunize our minds against sexism. A thinking environment is effectively a sexism-free zone.

SEXIST CONDITIONING:
ITS EFFECTS ON MEN

I agree with the person who said, 'If you could stack up these individual events and flip through them quickly, you would be able to see that being conditioned is actually an act of torture. And the installation of sexism is probably the most monstrous of all.'

I am not talking about men. Men are wonderful. I am talking about male conditioning. The two things are very different. Men, like women, are aware, full of life, relaxed, incisive, quick-witted, creative, generous and courageous. Male conditioning, on the other hand, is rigid, predatory, controlling and disconnected. Male conditioning is that set of messages that men must endure, believe and live out, in order to be seen as 'real men'. Male conditioning is destroying the world, and its first victims are men themselves. WAR

Women need to know the content of this conditioning and become skilled at recognizing it, playing victim to it no longer. One of our most insidious internal barriers is the way we confuse male conditioning with men themselves.

When we do, we obey the demands of the conditioning and hold back our excellence to protect male conditioning from embarrassment; we go quiet in the face of it; we watch our children being ravaged by it; we let it lower the standards of leadership for us; we beckon it into our beds for payment; and we assess our worth on the basis of its judgement of us. When we think that men and male conditioning are the same thing, we lose our power, and we abandon men in the process.

We can see that male conditioning is not the same as men because women can also suffer from it. I have worked with women who describe themselves much the way men do, saying that their childhood experience has many of the features of male conditioning. 'I was raised male,' one woman said to me. 'I can't feel a thing, I don't trust anyone, I use sex as a way to be close and then leave myself and my lover. I get my greatest satisfaction by outdoing others. I hate to admit to being wrong – I can't ask for directions when I am lost and so I get everybody more lost. I drink to let go, and I'd really rather fight than go to the trouble of working things out. Can you fix me?'

Some women who get to the very top of the towers of power in our society are women who are raised male. Some have said so, proudly. Twenty-seven years from now, when I hope women will have largely removed male conditioning from places of leadership and transformed them into good thinking environments, we may well look back at this era and say that the 'glass ceiling' was actually a blessing in disguise. Maybe we will see that it was really a fail-safe device, warning women to build more human and intelligent organizations as we rise, rather than sacrificing ourselves to the skeletons at the top of the old ones.

As women, we also need to stop relating to male conditioning and begin to relate to men as people, even when the conditioning is all we can see. Men are under there somewhere. The conditioning is vile. But men are fine.

We also need to provide a model of leadership that is not designed by male conditioning.

Women can begin to understand and defy male conditioning better if we see what it is like to live behind those bars. One way to do this is to consider what life would have been like for us as females if we had been conditioned with the messages men receive.

Even though not all men receive or absorb every one of these messages, and the onslaught is usually far more serious and brutal than women can imagine. Some women disbelieve the stories they hear about men's experience. Some women say that those things couldn't have happened, and surely did not happen to the men they know. But all too often they *do* happen, and men do not tell these stories even to their closest friends. Usually they don't think anyone would want to hear. Fortunately, Rosalind Miles has documented this conditioning process chillingly in her new book *Male Rites*.

So when we hear men talk about these experiences we must try to listen carefully. As women, we will be far more successful in eliminating sexism if we know the truth about this type of conditioning. Try, then, if you can, to imagine that as a child you were conditioned as men usually are. The picture below is a true one, drawn from what men have told me, not from my imagination. Try to imagine your childhood as if women, not men, were raised with male conditioning . . .

You were born. Everyone was thrilled that you were a girl. They celebrated you just because you were female.

In fact, from very early on in your life, you got the clear impression that the best thing to be was a girl and that the worst thing to be was a boy. Everyone became very nervous when you sounded or acted like a boy.

Most of all, it was unsettling to them when you cried. Sometimes they even hit you for crying which made you want to cry even more, and you had to learn as fast as possible how to make that pulsing hard lump in your throat go back down. Often they said things to you like, 'Stop crying at once. Girls don't cry. Only little boys cry and you wouldn't want anyone to call you a boy, now would you?'

Your eyes stung and your lips quivered, but eventually you learned how to stop. *Sometimes you could even manage not to feel anything and that made everything easier.*

They were eager for you to be seen as a 'woman' and even said things to each other in front of you like, 'Look at those little muscles. We've got to get her pumping iron.'

In this period, still young, you had a baby brother. Your parents spoke differently to him. They spoke softly and with more affection. They started calling you things like 'young woman' (though you were only six) while they called him 'sweetheart' and said 'I love you' all the time. They didn't hug you as often as they hugged him. They patted you on the head but cuddled you less and less.

Many of your toys were angular, hard and cold. They were high-speed things that crashed into other things. They were little women dressed for war. They were things you threw at other girls. They were long tubes you pointed at other girls and said, 'You're dead.' You couldn't talk to your toys very well or hold them close to you or be comforted by them.

Once you picked your best friend a bunch of flowers but she was disgusted when you gave them to her and called you a 'sissy'. The same thing happened when you said you wanted to try on your brother's ballet shoes – everyone seemed shocked.

And when you visited your friend and she said it would be fun to bake a cake together, her mother said something about how liberated little girls were getting these days. It was somehow exceptional and still not proper for little girls to do that. You did it anyway and enjoyed it, but something about it wasn't right. And you didn't do it again.

Your mother played with you now and then when she had time – usually outside, throwing things with you and kicking them. That's what she most liked to do with you and the better you got at kicking these things around, the happier she was with you. 'You're the best,' she would say, and pat you on the back.

As you got older, they rarely asked you how you were feeling. They liked it best when you didn't talk about that. Your brother, however, talked about his feelings most of the time.

The next year your friends started slapping each other on the back or the shoulder when they said hello. No one held hands or walked with their arms around each other any more. Instead, they started standing around with their hands in their pockets and tilting back on their heels to talk to each other. So did you. If you didn't, you knew that they would say things about your being a 'boy' and that they would leave you and laugh at you as they left. You had seen them do it to other girls.

Most of the magazine pictures you saw and films and ads you saw on TV showed women with muscles and stern faces and faraway looks in their eyes. The women rarely talked to each other except over a beer. And they never touched affectionately.

In fact, by the time you were eleven, girls weren't touching each other at all, except when their team beat another team of girls and then they could only punch each other's shoulders and slap palms.

One day you saw a girl walking from her father's car to the school building with her violin. You heard the jeers of the other girls in the playground and you decided you would never play an instrument. Some women did it, that was true, but your girlfriends said they were all 'poofs' who were in the orchestra and that was the same as being a man. You knew by now that if there was one thing you did not want to resemble, it was a man.

One day in the changing room – by now you were playing in three school teams – a group of other girls who were taller and bigger than you and who had pubic hair already and breasts and had even started their periods walked towards you with wet towels in their hands. They pointed at your bare vagina and little breasts and called you a wimp and then snapped the towels to graze and sting your legs. They backed you into a corner and you fell to the floor. They all stood around you calling you names and laughing. Then they left and you were alone.

It would be another year before your body changed and you would hate it all year. When you undressed from that point on, you felt sure there was something not right about the way your body looked even though it was more or less like everyone else's.

The next year you and some friends cornered a girl and stung her with towels. You felt slightly sick afterwards but didn't say so.

That same year you were getting changed for a football match and saw a group of senior girls standing around a short, fat girl with acne who was trying to pull up her underwear underneath a towel to hide her body. You laughed, too.

But you didn't really like it, not any more than you liked putting shaving cream and vaseline and diet plans in her locker at school the next day, or peeing on her books along with the other girls. But you did it.

Soon your attention was drawn back to boys. You were supposed to like them. Your friends talked about them constantly. What they said was that boys and men 'were there for you to fuck', and time was running out for you to prove that you could do it. Some of your friends had already 'scored',

38

had had three or four boys even, and one girl had had twelve, she said. You didn't know how to get a boy to agree to 'do it' and none of the girls would tell you what they did. The idea was just to get it, even if the boys didn't want to give it. They said the boy really did want to give it, anyway, even if he said no all the time you were doing it to him.

The other girls also told you that sex was a stronger drive in you than in boys. There was nothing you could do about this drive, and when your vagina started to tingle because a man walked by or looked at you, it was his fault. It was probably the sexy way he was dressed, and you could blame him and expect him to do whatever you wanted.

You began to look at magazines with pictures of naked men who looked wistful and weak and you felt the tingling in your vagina again. Sometimes you stuck these pictures inside your school locker. Real women did that.

It seemed as if everything physically pleasurable was supposed to lead to sex and that you were supposed to overpower the man while you did it. In fact, the idea seemed to be for the man to throw his head back in uncontrollable ecstasy just because you were there, no matter what you were doing, taking a Power Shower, eating a Flake or sunning with Ambre Solaire. There didn't seem to be much difference.

And when you looked at men and boys, even in academic classes or meetings, you began to imagine them naked and in bed with you. That was all right because what they had to say in class and in meetings wasn't particularly important anyway.

As you got older, you kept hearing, even though no one was exactly saying it, that you were supposed to control everything, to be the best at whatever it was, not to make mistakes, and to know that that would mean outdoing other women.

Other women, in fact, would be a problem. You couldn't be sure what they might do to show you up. The woman next to you might be your friend one minute and plot against you the next to try to be 'the best' herself and to outdo you, so you would have to be one up on her whenever possible. To lose would be a sign of diminished womanhood. To be a real woman *was to win. Nothing should distract you from that.*

You were beginning to understand that in the end everything would be up to you, you would probably have to earn all the money for the family when you were grown up, make all the major decisions, and, without asking why, hand over your life for your country if the other women running it should decide to go to war.

You stopped talking to women about your problems except over a drink, and when you were twenty-five you noticed that it had been years since you had cried. It was some consolation, though, that no one had ever called you a man.

It was unequivocal that you were not to be scared, even in war, and that if you ever were, you were never to say so. Your greatest fear was of fear.

You had to be willing and ready to fight other women. The first time you hit another girl, it had been hard, but the next time wasn't so bad. Girls had beaten you up, your face and eyes and fists had ached and bled on many occasions. You had learned that real women solve most problems this way.

And you knew, without having to hear it in so many words, that the most glorious, most womanly thing you could do in your life would be, in the name of honour, to kill other women.

If you had been conditioned this way, how would you feel about other women? How would you feel about yourself? And how would you lead? Try to answer these questions; discuss them with a friend if you can, before you read on.

I remember hearing a young father say, holding his tiny baby son, who was screaming as infants do, 'You stop it, stop it, do you hear? By God, no son of mine is going to act like a sissy! And you'd better get used to that, starting now.' He threw him on the bed and left the room slamming the door. The baby's mother raced up the stairs and took the baby in her arms. The father shouted from below, 'You're making a fucking poof out of that kid. No poof is going to live in this house!'

The mother ignored the father and comforted her son. She told me later, the terror still controlling her face, that she was grateful he hadn't thrown him on the floor. I wondered to myself how long it would be before he would.

This is sexist conditioning for men. This is torture. Fortunately, not every man receives a full dose, and some men resist its effects admirably. There are men who hate this conditioning and defy it every day, contributing their intelligence, humanity and creativity to our world. But it is pervasive and brutal enough to account for many of the hurtful, counter-productive, unreasonable things men do. It goes a long way towards explaining why a thinking environment is so rare in our mostly male-conditioned organizations. In a funny way, this should give us hope because it means that rigid male behaviour is not genetically induced and can, therefore, eventually be changed.

I have yet to find a woman who can begin to imagine the constant eroding pain this conditioning inflicts on men and how early the process begins for them. When we think about it we feel sick. I have often said that I would rather be a woman reclaiming my power than a man reclaiming my humanity.

Convulsing under male conditioning, the human mind cannot take a broad perspective, manage ambiguity, change its frame of reference, celebrate the joys and successes of others, reach out tenderly or open itself to the cause beneath the surface. It struggles with interactive thinking.

No wonder our companies and organizations, our political and social structures, our laws, policies and economic systems are so often unworkable or harmful. Many of them were produced by male conditioning.

Male conditioning, instilled with violence and absorbed in obedience, makes men consider violence as the first solution to conflict. In this sense, sexism is a cause of war.

As a society we need to acknowledge this brutalization of men, and then think carefully about whether we wish to continue it. The danger is that, once it is in place, it takes time to remove, because the victims, the men themselves, begin to defend it. They can no longer see that men's conditioning is not men's nature. They can no longer conceive of a fuller, deeper, better way to think.

They are terrified to consider another way of thinking because it will mean becoming like women. And this they want to avoid at all costs. They would rather remain cornered by the pincer movement of sexism than claim for themselves the thinking and behaviour they associate with women. Even when we describe how good it is to be free of their shackles, they shudder at the thought of being like us. And inside the conditioning they conspire to silence us and to entice us to lead the way they do.

As in Plato's allegory, male conditioning 'kills' the person who, having ventured outside the pitch dark of the cave, comes back to report that there is such a thing as light.

SEXIST CONDITIONING IN PRACTICE

From my earliest childhood I was aware of the brutality done to boys to turn them into 'real men'. I have a twin brother and we were treated very differently – the same parents, the same house, the same amount of love, but very different messages. Bill was treated as a little man and encouraged to play with guns and cars and footballs and model aeroplanes. I had wonderful dolls and domestic toys and musical instruments and skipping ropes. I was allowed to play with his things if I wanted to but he was not to be seen playing with anything of mine, particularly dolls. All his books were adventure stories about men conquering nature. Mine were stories about people helping each other. Even our birthday cakes were different. My cake was designed as a maypole with lovely streamers and little girls dancing together. His was a baseball pitch with men defeating each other.

When he misbehaved, he had to wait all day for Dad's arrival and punishment. The wait and their 'time alone' were agony for me. I never knew what went on, and I never saw Bill cry.

Over the years his temper got shorter and he didn't want to talk about loving me any more. I did not understand. I thought there must be something wrong with me.

Somehow I knew this was all hard on Mother, even though she allowed it. I remember a special kind of pain in her face when Dad yelled at Bill and frightened him. I always wondered where Mother put that pain. One day she and I were walking down the hall past Bill's room. He was sleeping, and she peeped in and just looked at him. As we walked on, she said, 'There isn't an unkind bone in his body,' and she squeezed my hand. Her attention went far away.

I think my most poignant memory of his conditioning was the day we left him at military school. He and I were fifteen years old. All five of the family had driven the hundred miles to take him to his new school. Just a few hours before he was due at the school, we were swimming in a nearby hotel pool. We were watching Bill dive, and as his body came out of the air, his head grazed the diving board. We heard the crack and, as his body hit the water, we saw the blood. Dad jumped into the pool fully dressed and pulled him to the edge and out. At the hospital they said Bill would eventually be all right, but that he should rest, and that he was lucky not to have concussion. They bandaged his head in white gauze.

But within three hours he was at the school. The commanders gave him his uniform, shaved his head, and showed him to his sleeping quarters. He was given an hour to learn the rules and regulations.

While he did this, we wandered round the grounds. I thought the trees were pretty and hoped Bill would be allowed to sit under them to study as I was at my school.

At 5 o'clock families were told to leave. The officials said the boys would be allowed to say goodbye. We rushed back to the car and waited for Bill. Shortly a small boy, almost swallowed by an army coat and pants, in a hat with white gauze showing just underneath, appeared in the distance and walked towards our car. Resting against his shoulder, looking nearly as big as him, was an M1 rifle.

Dad got out of the car. Bill stood to attention as Dad approached. I started to get out. More than anything in the world, I wanted to hug Bill. But Mother said firmly, 'No, we mustn't. He wouldn't want us to. It would not be right for the women to . . .' I didn't hear the rest of what she said.

Dad stepped closer to him. I saw Bill's eyes reaching. Dad's body seemed tentative and tender, and I knew it would all be better when they hugged goodbye. But Dad held out his hand. Bill looked down. He moved his hand towards Dad's. I wanted to scream, 'Grab him, Bill, make him hug you. He is sad, too.' But their hands met in a clasp and a shake.

Dad then turned back to the car and motioned to Mother to come. *I* wanted to come but she said no. So I prayed she would take Bill in her arms and whisper to him to call home any time and tell him it was OK if he felt homesick and that he would probably cry a lot and that soon it would be better and that they would be proud of him no matter what and that the first year is tough and that average grades would be fine, just as they had done with me the year before at my school.

Mother stood waiting. She looked at him and he at her. His forehead creased and he blinked. I saw tears. She waited. Then he stretched out his hand, and she shook it.

On the way to dinner I was inconsolable and so was my sister. I cried and cried and cried. Uncharacteristically defiant, I kept crying even as Mother and Dad tried to hush me. I could not put it into words then. But I knew that what I had just witnessed was violence and that every one of us had been hurt. What it would take me years to work out was why none of us had been able to stop it. I would not understand about women's conditioning until much later.

This happened thirty years ago. That generation is now beginning to fill top leadership positions in the world. In the next ten years they will be fully in charge of what happens to our planet.

With the younger generations, things are only marginally better. The systematic brutalizing of boys goes on. You can see it all around you.

Just last month I was having breakfast with Meghan, my six-year-old god-daughter. Her three-year-old brother was racing round the house with his hands stretched out in front of him, making ack-ack sounds like a machine gun.

'Why is he doing that?' I asked her.

'Oh, you know boys,' she said.

'Really?' I asked, impressed with a feminist analysis from this six-year-old.

'Yeah, boys do that stupid stuff.'

'Well, why do you think they do?' I said.

'I don't know,' she said. 'They all sit around watching it on the videos and then they do it to each other. That's all I can tell you.'

Understanding the process of male conditioning will help us take steps to reduce it, and stop it when we can. It will help make sense of, though never excuse, the things men do while controlled by their conditioning. It may also help us see that women, who are generally encouraged to think more interactively and feel more accurately, should be leading as soon as possible.

As women, we can remove the barriers that hold us back and regain our power, day by day, in thinking partnerships with each other. Then, as we lead, men will eventually seek out our culture. They will ask to live in it with us – and their conditioning will eventually give way. We cannot help men by putting all our energies into trying to change them. We can help them by leading them until they follow us back to their humanity.

SEXIST CONDITIONING:
ITS EFFECTS ON WOMEN

Women are not psychological spectators in this massacre called sexism. We are made to participate in it through our conditioning as well. Female conditioning does not inflict damage on our humanity, but it does convince us that we are powerless to stop the carnage around us. It also convinces us that our superb interactive thinking skills are of limited value, and so we do not assert them as thinking leaders to reverse the destruction caused by sexism. Through our conditioning, we watch, we ache, we look away, we obey, and we eventually agree to revere and follow the distortions of male conditioning.

Men will follow us back to their humanity.

I used to think that women no longer needed to articulate the messages of female conditioning. Surely we know them by now, and understand how they slip like silverfish into our dreams and silently eat them alive. But I have found that, even for seasoned career women and campaigners, a periodic look into the face of our conditioning can bring new insights and strengthen the weak links in our resolve.

If you were asked to make a list of the messages women receive about what real women are (whether you believe them or not), what would you say? In my work with women I have grown accustomed to seeing virtually the same list of stereotypes over and over again, regardless of the women's country, their culture, or their age. Twelve-year-old women make essentially the same list as seventy-year-old women.

One young woman suggested that we make four lists: one with the lies of our conditioning, one with the way those lies make us feel, one with the way those feelings make us act, and one with the facts about women and men. A typical list is on pages 46 and 47.

This conditioning still influences almost every female's view of herself and her world. Many women have fought and won on some of these issues, and young women in some countries today are encouraged not to believe all these stereotypes. But even in our most gender-liberated societies some of these messages still take up residence in our brains and help to explain why 52 per cent of the population makes up only 8 per cent of the world's leadership. The struggle goes on, even in the most outwardly liberated lives.

The first step in ridding ourselves of this conditioning is to admit that it affects us. Go back for a moment to the four women's conditioning columns. Read through the lists and pick out one message of sexism that you still struggle with in yourself.

Then make a decision to give up that message. What would you do differently in your life if you no longer believed that message and no longer let it influence your decisions?

We must stop kidding ourselves. Sexism is not dead.

The lies of our conditioning are the biggest barrier to our power. When we recognize this and assert our female culture proudly, we may then, while continuing to shed our negative female conditioning, provide some of the best leadership the world has ever known.

Lies About Women (Conditioning)	How The Lies Make Us Feel
Women are illogical.	Ungrounded, naive.
Women are weak.	Helpless, dependent, vulnerable.
Women are unreliable with money.	Uncertain when money is the topic. Undeserving of reasonable rates of pay.
Women are indecisive.	Powerless, blocked, scattered, confused.
Women cause unbidden sexual feelings in men.	Responsible for men's sexual behaviour.
What women want is less important than what men want.	Out of touch with our own needs and ideas.
Women are too emotional.	Ashamed of our emotions.
Women don't discuss; they gossip.	Stupid.
Women should not have sole say over their own bodies.	Unsafe, out of control, compliant.
A woman's main goal in life is to be loved by a man.	Obsessed with what men think of us.
The female body is beautiful only if it looks a certain way.	Critical of our bodies. Ashamed, uncertain.
Women are good with children and not good in public decision-making roles.	Incompetent in adult spheres of influence.
Women are intuitive and thus mysterious and dangerous.	Insubstantial, unreal.
Women cannot lead.	Trapped, victimized and obedient.

How The Feelings Make Us Act	Facts About Women and Men
Hide our thinking. Avoid public debate.	Women and men are equally logical.
Limit our physical development. Remain in abusive relationships.	Women have greater physical endurance than men, have greater energy reserves, adapt better to extremes of temperature, have 60 per cent more strength in their thighs, replace blood more quickly, breathe more often, survive accidents more often and survive starvation, exposure, fatigue, shock and illness better than men.
Give away financial decision-making power to men.	Family finances are run successfully more often by women than by men. Before sexist conditioning takes root, girls score higher in maths than boys of the same age.
Defer to men's decisions. Do too many things at once.	In the home and workplace women make more decisions than men. Women's ability to consult widely produces better executive decisions.
Say yes when we mean no. Don't report abuse.	Men choose to feel sexual and can decide not to at any given moment.
Focus on pleasing men. Hold back our own leadership abilities.	What women want is often the missing element needed for advanced solutions to problems.
Deny the horrors that exist.	People who have easy access to their emotions think more clearly and see from more perspectives. Male and female babies show no difference in their ability or proclivity to cry.
Falter in intellectual conversation. Flirt.	Men gossip more than women. There is no difference in male and female intellectual capacity.
Practise unsafe sex. Bear unwanted children. Agree to abuse. Neglect ourselves. Die.	A woman's body is her own and no one else's.
Hold back for fear of outshining men. Say no to leadership.	Women and men both need to be loved and to contribute to society. Women are complete without men.
Spend time and money trying to look different. Seek the background, not the spotlight.	All female bodies are beautiful. Health, not appearance, is the legitimate drive for change.
Censor dreams of public power.	Men and women are inherently equally good with children and in leadership positions.
Speak vaguely. Not take ourselves seriously. Censor ourselves.	More than 80 per cent of intuited information is correct. Women and men demonstrate equal intuitive ability.
Manipulate, blame and resent men in power. Hold ourselves back from key public roles.	Women lead all day, every day. Women's in-tact interactive thinking can make them particularly good leaders.

CHAPTER 4

Who is Encouraged to Think?

In West London there is a voluntary organization employing 500 people in a mix of paid and unpaid positions. It is called London Lighthouse. It comes closer than any organization I've known to being a thinking environment. The ten components of a thinking environment are the basis of their structures and of their personal interactions.

One of their written policies, for example, is that every employee receives an hour and a half per week of support group time. People meet together in groups of four or five to take turns *listening* to each other or doing whatever will *encourage* them to continue to function well in the organization. Everyone is entitled to this hour and a half as part of their worktime; the organization sees it as part of what keeps people thinking well.

The largest residential and support centre in the world, for people affected by HIV and AIDS the Lighthouse is a place where people of diverse backgrounds, groups and identities are *appreciated*. As one staff member told me, 'Appreciating each other here is very, very, very important. From the minute you walk in you are faced with the some-times disturbing fact that you matter profoundly.'

People can feel it even as they walk into the *physical environment* of the building. In fact, the building was itself designed to reflect the philosophy of the organization. Its corridors are wide; its colours are terracotta and blue and cream, as if nature itself had done the painting. Glass wells and bridges pour light down three floors from the residential unit to reception, linking people and departments, and reducing isolation. The front entrance reaches right out to the street, and – like much of the building – curves, embraces and doesn't rush.

The architect said of his design, 'I was determined to transform the building into a place of safety and comfort for peopled affected by AIDS. I was aware of the need to use materials that would make people feel valued.'

The project also asks *incisive questions*, not only of staff and users, but also of the global community coming to grips with the multiple issues AIDS raises in everyone's life. One resounding question it asks the world is, 'If your organization could look into the face of death every day, how would it improve the quality of life there?'

A different but equally important question it poses is, 'If you could have the best for the people you serve, what would it be and what would have to change for it to take place?'

Sometimes a candle burns on the desk at reception. This means that someone has died the night before. And it is not uncommon then to see people with their arms around each other, one person crying a bit, the other listening. *Feelings* of other sorts are also allowed here. The work can be exhausting, the circumstances can be frightening – most of which people can talk about and face with each other's understanding. This is done in various ways and does not impede or diminish the work being done. In fact people say their work improves because they are able to express the way they feel.

The most delicate aspect of maintaining a thinking environment in a large organization is the balancing of *boundaries* and *equality*. The Lighthouse keeps trying to find that balance. The director, managers and staff are generally accessible to each other as equal partners in thinking sessions and meetings, including in a consultative forum which is an elected representative group to review any issue and suggest change.

At the same time, the lines of authority are clear, the boundaries of job descriptions, legal responsibilities and decision-making are agreed upon and respected. This seems to allow for maximum creativity in developing the project, and maximum efficiency in running it.

Building a thinking environment in an organization is far more difficult than building a single thinking partnership with one other person. One reason for the Lighthouse's success in doing this may be the fact that it has turned away from male conditioning as a model for leadership and turned instead towards the humanness and flexibility associated with women's culture. As organizations develop in this way, I believe they will become environments in which people can truly think together and in which work is generally fulfilling. They will also become places in which institutional sexism and oppression can be dramatically reduced and in which individuals can help each other remove internal barriers to their power and effectiveness.

GOVERNMENT

I would like to see governments turn in this direction as well. Consider the British Parliament, for example. There is probably no institution with a more impassioned or earnest workforce, nor one with worthier stated aims. But Parliament's goals are rarely reached because it has to struggle every day against systemic difficulty in creating a thinking environment.

Any Tuesday or Thursday during Prime Minister's Questions, for example, virtually every one of the ten components of a thinking environment is compromised.

The issues are aired in the form, not of real *questions* and certainly not of incisive ones, but of prepared questions and answers and then of attack in the guise of questions.

Members rarely *listen*. In fact, most of the time almost everyone is talking, mumbling, moaning or shouting at each other. In the process they are doing everything they can do to drown out the person speaking.

Apart from partisan cheering, it is rare for anyone to show *appreciation*. As a rule, the ratio of appreciation to criticism is probably less than one to ten. There are relentless direct assaults on the members speaking, attitudes are rudely dismissive or aggressive, and ridicule and withering tones of voice are everywhere, forcing him (usually) to climb over boulders of abuse, lucky to hold on to his idea at all, never mind develop a new one.

Encouragement does not seem to be relevant here either. The point is to win, not to create something new.

Equality, too, seems to be explicitly banned from Parliament. Everything in the room speaks of rank and order and place. 'Backbenchers', 'the Right Honourable Members', the Speaker's wig and robe, all say he is better than she is better than he is. . . . Status, not thinking, prevails in the House.

Nor can you find *diversity* in Parliament. It is heavily dominated by white able-bodied older heterosexual men who earn above average incomes. Who can think afresh in such a sea of homogeneity?

Boundaries are constantly invaded by the nature of party political debate. The thinking process is neutralized by loyalty to party policy.

And *feelings*? We do find feelings in Parliament, but in exactly the ways that destroy a thinking environment. The person speaking doesn't have the time or attention to examine their feelings well enough to separate them from their ideas. At the same time the listeners are hurling their feelings across the room, right into the path of the person speaking, virtually all the time. The most acceptable feeling seems to be that of pompous outrage. Very little real feeling is permissible and so nothing very real has a chance of surfacing, whether in feeling or thought.

The *physical environment* of Parliament is another obstacle. Long hard benches in rows are conducive to rhetoric, to ridicule, to ritual, and occasionally to rationalization, but not to reason. They isolate people. No one is intended to interact here. Promote themselves, yes. Dismiss their opponents, yes. Follow a rigid structure, yes. Think, no.

And Parliament is certainly not the place to ask for genuine *information*. If you do, you are called unprepared or incompetent, if you're lucky. As for accurate information about your shortcomings, that is so mixed up with gratuitous insults that you gain no helpful personal insights. And new positive information about yourself is nowhere to be heard. You hang on by your fingernails to what you already had when you walked in, if you can.

Attack and defence are the two components of Parliament. Neither belongs in a thinking environment.

This would all be tolerable if it were a school sporting activity (which is where these ways of behaving are first practised and learned). But it is not. It is a decision-making process that affects millions of lives.

It is even more shocking that most Members will probably tell you they enjoy the sparring, the cut and thrust of parliamentary debate, and they will defend it as the heart of democracy. A thinking environment is the heart of democracy. Sport is just sport.

I like the question: 'If government were restructured in all its aspects to be a thinking environment, how would it change?' I immediately wonder how long it would take then to get 300 women to stand for and win seats in Parliament. Not many of us at this point are willing to display our minds and hearts in the House that way and at the end of our lives wonder if we have done something worthwhile. A real thinking environment, on the other hand, would appeal to most women. Then the country could more nearly realize the democratic aims of Parliament and more nearly offer real leadership to the people.

SCHOOLS

It is one thing when government ministers fail to create a thinking environment, but for schools to fail in this way seems to me an outrage. By their very nature, schools should be thinking environments. But which of the ten components are present in a typical student's day? No matter what their age, or the level of study they are engaged in, students are rarely treated to a thinking environment.

Teachers aren't trained in these skills. They impart information, often beautifully. They evaluate students' responses, often fairly and compassionately. They frequently provoke lively, rigorous discussion. They open up intellectual and aesthetic worlds. But they rarely get students to think for themselves, without inhibition.

Too often students learn that they must concentrate on being correct rather than imaginative. They are judged on how they compare with other students, not on how they compare with their previous performance. They are, on occasion, publicly shamed, even hit, for mistakes and are made to question their own inborn intelligence. They are hardly ever taught the skills of a thinking environment. The 'thinking' they are encouraged to do is too often more a cross between regurgitation and obfuscation.

Of the few students who continue to love thinking or who even remember how to think after they leave school, most will tell you that the most stimulating times for them were when they were on their own, outside the classroom or laboratory. When computer companies go to university campuses to find the brightest new ideas for computer technology, for example, they usually find them among students working passionately and independently on their own, not among those who are simply following the curriculum. Even as a child I remember wondering what had gone so wrong in the school system that Einstein had failed mathematics.

On one of my visits to a university I witnessed a sobering incident. I had stopped in to visit a colleague who taught there. We were just leaving her office when a student appeared sheepishly from behind a marble pillar, having waited nearly an hour to see this professor.

'Oh, what are you doing here, Amanda?' my friend asked.

'I need to talk to you if you have a minute, Dr Montgomery,' she answered.

'My office hours were up two hours ago,' the professor said.

Amanda looked at the floor.

'Well, all right, what is it about?'

'It is about my paper topic for the Hopi mythology course. I have a good idea and I need your approval.'

'Excuse me, Nancy,' Dr Montgomery snapped. 'Amanda, come into my office. If you had been in class today you would have received my list of suggested paper topics and we wouldn't have to do this.'

Amanda continued to look at her professor. She opened her mouth with resolve but with obvious effort. 'I want to consider the Hopi origin myth in the light of Levi Strauss's theory of the dialectic in the development of culture.'

The professor squinted. 'What makes you think you could manage that, Amanda? How much experience have you had in crossing two different disciplines? One is, as you surely know, a form of literature, and the other a social theory.'

'I know. In fact that's what excites me. I think I can find the dialectic in the Hopi origin myth,' she answered.

Amanda was holding her own. At that moment the professor had the perfect opportunity to help her by creating a thinking environment. But Dr Montgomery said, 'Well, now, Amanda, judging from the last paper you wrote and from your last exam I would say that we wouldn't want to take any chances with you. You'd better do whatever possible to bring that grade up. I'd strongly recommend that you stick with my suggested list of paper topics. We wouldn't want to have the same débâcle we had last term, now would we?'

End of thinking – not one of the ten components to be found anywhere. Whatever ideas Amanda had generated were now pulp. The colour left her face and the little bit of light that had been in her eyes dimmed away. She looked down at Dr Montgomery's list of topics. 'No, I guess we wouldn't, Dr Montgomery. OK. Thank you.' And she walked away.

Dr Montgomery and I left the office and locked the door. As we walked down the empty hall, my silence no doubt betraying my horror at what I had just seen, she said, 'You know, you just have to save them from themselves sometimes.'

Schools don't mean to, but they can silence students. Too many schools control, punish, mould and frighten students. And many who survive only do so by developing a sense of their own superiority and then, like their teachers before them, they become isolated from a vast range of human experience. Only concerned to receive endorsement from their equally isolated peers, they soon stop thinking. Possession of knowledge – some of it arcane – and agreed-upon performance levels are the acknowledged aims in most schools. Genuine exploration, consultation and collaboration – the hallmarks of real thinking – are not.

There are, fortunately, some exceptions. At the age of twenty-five, Ivan Battle founded a music academy for young people. He believed that, under certain conditions, young people could learn how to play the piano as if they were virtuosos. His record of state competition results seems to bear this out. I asked him how he did it.

'We love the children,' he said.

I asked him to explain what he meant by this.

'We praise them,' he said. 'We point out everything we can possibly find that is good before we say what needs improvement.

'Before we start the lesson, we ask students to share the difficulties of their day and even the ongoing struggles of their life. We don't take for ever on this, but we do make sure they can unload some of their troubles because their minds are freer to create and to learn if they do. And it helps them relax to know that we care about them as people, not just as performers. Even at the age of six this affects their learning.

'After we get to know the students a bit, we choose pieces for them to learn that will stretch the less developed sides of their personalities, pieces that will show them strengths they didn't think they had. For example, one of my students came to us very angry and unsure of herself. She was limited by the unspent hostility she felt toward her parents and her former teachers. So I had her learn 'The Jeering Song' by Bartok to express the intensity of her feelings. I told her to go home and pound out that piece until she could get past the anger she felt. She did, and soon the intensity became power. Then it was time to balance the power with the beauty in her. So I gave her John Field's 'Nocturne' to learn. Gradually she has begun to play everything with more authenticity than before because she is playing with more of herself.

'We help them to see that they are clever and talented, and then we require high levels of performance from them. They learn faster and faster. In state-wide competition, most of them outstrip other students of their age and experience. I'd still say that what we do is love them.'

Without calling it that, Ivan has created a thinking environment in his academy. I visited one day and saw his philosophy in action. He really did what he said, and the students played superbly. All ten components were present during the lesson I observed. And the effect showed, not only in the quality of the students' playing, but on their faces, too. I agree with Ivan. Love is a good word for a thinking environment.

CHAPTER 5

Motherhood: Consider It Leadership

'It is as if you wrap your arms around the organization and think.' In a team meeting recently the director of a voluntary organization said this of the senior assistant. The director told her that one of the reasons the organization works well is that she treats the people and the projects in very much the same way as she relates to the children in her life, that she enables people to know their value and to think well together and to have the courage to make far-reaching changes even if they are controversial.

She was pleased to be seen in that way, and to have her mothering skills linked to her managerial skills. She said, 'I've known for years that they are one and the same thing but as a feminist I've never dared say so. It is a relief now not to have to file my knowledge under B for baby and lock the drawer.'

Most women become mothers. This time-consuming and essential work has usually been categorized in two ways. It has either been seen as the *only* thing women are designed by nature to do, or it has been something that career and professional women should do in the background and on the run. Neither extreme is right. Rather, motherhood is one of many leadership roles women can choose to develop in their lifetime.

Our biology determines that we have babies. But it does not determine how much status that job has in our society. Sexism does that. There is nothing wrong with motherhood. There is something wrong with the oppression that has marginalized it.

I believe that when mothering is given the status of leadership work, we will be able to improve leadership in general, making it more consistent with the human values required in mothering. And women, recognized for the leadership they have developed as mothers, will lead in the world in much greater numbers. The marginalization of motherhood has held leadership back from its human potential and women back from their potential leadership.

MOTHERHOOD AND
LEADERSHIP THINKING

The particular expertise I am talking about is the ability to do all *three kinds of leadership thinking at once:* interactive thinking, structural thinking and promotional thinking. It is in being prepared for motherhood, in using all three kinds of thinking at once, that women may actually be preparing for high-level leadership in the world. Men, on the other hand, do not in their culture or boyhood play have a job or role that requires them to practise all three kinds of thinking simultaneously. Men are encouraged to think promotionally and structurally but they are not expected to think interactively as well.

MOTHERS AS INTERACTIVE THINKERS

In Chapter Three I suggested ten ways human beings think interactively. To do her job well, a mother has to think *interactively* all the time.

1　She has to care about the way her children are thinking, feeling and reacting, keeping in mind the whole picture of their lives and well-being with every decision she makes.
2　She must bring disparate elements together and come up with new ideas all day long.
3　She must keep the whole picture in mind while also focusing on the details.
4　She must value ideas because they work, not because of who has endorsed them.
5　She must manage ambiguity, holding the truth of several conflicting things at once.

6 She must repeatedly remove the barriers in her child's mind, seeing new possibilities with every situation.

7 In conflict, she must care more about the integrity of the outcome than about her emotionally invested preference for resolution.

8 She must see issues from many perspectives.

9 She must identify the key thing which will change everything else, being an expert in efficiency.

10 She must find out what really happened in an event in her child's day, constantly taking her own head out of the sand of denial and wishful thinking.

11 She must look relentlessly for the big issues below the surface, knowing that 'where there is a tip there is an iceberg'.

MOTHERS AS PROMOTIONAL THINKERS

Also, mothering is the main area of women's traditional culture in which *promotional* thinking is taught and reinforced. Women are not generally encouraged to promote themselves. We are made to feel best while promoting others. We often experience discomfort, in fact, when we are too much in the glare of publicity. Even publicly prominent women tend to set a limit on how far they will promote themselves. When their limited internal image of themselves no longer matches the external requirement, they stop. Getting women to keep stepping forward with their own ideas and skills is a major task for us as we try to increase the number of women in leadership.

But women who have been mothers, and women who in girlhood pretended to be mothers, have an excellent reference point for the interface of promotional and interactive thinking. We have practised it for years with our children. We have felt at ease promoting our ideas, our values, our plans, proposals, points of view and policies with our children all day every day. With children, mothers can be the ultimate authority and the central influence. While mothering, women usually feel quite comfortable with promotional thinking. Mothering has become a reference point for use in expressing this aspect of leadership behaviour. Now we need to use it comfortably beyond our family, in the larger world of leadership.

MOTHERS AS STRUCTURAL THINKERS

To do her job well, a mother must think *structurally*, too. And her structural thinking skills would easily rival those of any company manager. When in top form she can be found organizing a vast multiplicity of activities and appointments: meals, transport arrangements, play and sleep; the overlapping, dovetailing, and often conflicting schedules of many people, emergencies, routine needs and intermittent appointments. She is in charge of many long-term projects and succeeds in meeting hundreds of short-term targets. She balances everyone's work with necessary rest and recreation, and she organizes community activities. She delegates, scrutinizes, trains, and processes information. She keeps accounts and reports, and maintains a strong managerial focus while developing team skills among those she oversees. Hearing the strategies, calibre of thinking, negotiating, hiring and firing, balancing, prioritizing, budgeting, deciding, training, inspiring and policy development that go on in the day of even one mother, you will usually hear a day in the life of a leader.

In just the thirty or so minutes before children leave for school, for example, she will not untypically have to make fifteen management decisions. They can include what she and the children will wear so that everyone is warm enough and looks appropriate; whether or not to read another paragraph of a story to her child when he is due at school in fifteen minutes; whether the person she loves most in the world will be defiant or grateful if she brings up the subject of their health again; whether they can afford to go to the seaside for a week; whether or not giving a present to one person to celebrate a success will make another one feel like a failure; how to get more fibre into the packed lunches her family will take that day; whom she can trust to mind the children every Wednesday afternoon; which political party in the forthcoming election offers the best manifesto for her children's needs; how to get the teachers to take a more co-ordinated approach to the problem her child is having at school; what to serve for dinner so that everyone will eat; which bills to pay now and which to leave; whether to listen again or give advice; how to start saying no when for years she's said yes. All this before 7:30. And this is just about her mothering; never mind the floods of decisions she will be juggling at the same time about her paid work, her relationships and her own health. She is no stranger to the requirements of executive decision-making.

Of course, not all mothers do these things all the time and they do not all do them with consistent excellence. At one and the same time, mothers can be the most competent and inspiring leaders and the most destructive. As with any leadership role, there is always plenty of room for mistakes, and failures go with the territory. I am not trying to say that mothers are saints, and the minute they have brought up a child they automatically become perfect leaders, ready to be launched into any leadership position in the world. The point is that, while women are mothering, they are probably practising vital leadership skills and that experience should be seen and valued as such by society. When we do recognize mothering as leadership experience, women will seek leadership in the wider world with more confidence, they will bring to leadership the interactive thinking skills that are often missing in male-conditioned leadership, and women will probably also do an even better job of mothering. Convincing women, and the world, that motherhood is leadership is the hard part.

GETTING MOTHERHOOD
INTO LEADERSHIP

Many women are saying these days that a strong women's presence at the top (women not conditioned as men, that is) can change for the better many things organizations and leaders do. Female company directors are often described as being changers of organizational culture. Studies of businesses that have been founded and run by women bear out the notion that women who stay true to themselves, as they run a company, lead more often by empowering others than by dominating them. The cultures of their companies are described by researchers like Judy Rosener as more open, more participatory, transformative, inclusive and creative. Job satisfaction is high and profits stay high as well. Women are reporting a similar cultural change in the political campaigns of women candidates.

The message that the time women spend as mothers is always time off from leadership is a lie and can be a big barrier for women as they dare to contemplate moving into public and professional leadership roles. True, women who have not been mothers also make good leaders – it is not just the act of bringing up a child but also women's cultural reinforcement in the thinking skills necessary to do so that is important. And, true, we mustn't idealize motherhood and let it become a one-way trip back into the feminine mystique or an escape from public leadership. But we must also recognize it as leadership in itself, to be listed on our CVs along with Chair, Director, and President of this, that and the other.

My friend Amy said it well: 'I don't want to use mothering, which is more comfortable for me, as a retreat from the challenge of public leadership in the world, but I must also recognize that motherhood is one branch of professional leadership – both are true. I have to live with the discomfort of that paradox.'

After I finished one of the drafts of this chapter, I asked a friend of mine, a young mother of three, to read it and comment on it for me. She did, and left me this note:

. . . How did you know this? This is why mothering is hard work, not just because of the physical aspects, but because of all the influential and emotional development aspects, too. And they happen not just once, as with one child, but twice, three times, even more for some women. The children are all so individual and thus need individual attention on all levels.

You have put into words what I have subsconsciously known. It is a pleasure to see that a mother can have a rightful place in society, can be a person of importance. If I felt that I could run a job, a career, a business as well as I run the children, our home and our lives, I would want to go into the world and continue to give and grow and be fulfilled as I have over the last eight years with the children, never stopping but reaching higher and further.

But realistically I worry that this is not possible. I never thought that motherhood and leadership could compare, but I hope and pray they do.

Julie

I believe that there is a public leader waiting to be acknowledged and developed inside her. Recognition by her and the world that her mothering and the act of leading *do* compare would go a long way towards unveiling that leader.

FATHERHOOD: IS IT LEADERSHIP?

If mothers are leaders, aren't fathers, too? Yes. But so far only occasionally. A few fathers lead with their children the way mothers traditionally do. That is important because it is another demonstration that men are inherently just as competent at interactive thinking skills as women.

But the norm is the man, controlled by his conditioning, who lives with a woman and expects her to run the home, bring up the children, look after him, and work outside the home as well. Too often, still, he collapses in front of the TV after work and demands a beer as reward for a hard day.

There is some increase in the number of men 'doing childcare'. But that is not the same as being a leader in caring for a child. The childcare father does not have to take a constant overview of the children's life and growth, structure his diary every day around their needs, understand the complex human relations in their lives or the subtleties of their emotional struggles, or think about the quality of their family life. He may cook a meal or wash a load of laundry or settle an argument or read a story to the children every night. But he does not oversee their long-term health, or maintain a domestic system of cleanliness, use of space, and family relations. He may drive his daughter on occasion to her netball practice or agree to put the paper down to hear his son play the tune he has just learnt on his flute, but he does not think about the child's whole physical, artistic, social, medical, emotional or academic development and consider what should be done to enhance it year after year. And usually he is not the one who gets up in the middle of the night.

He helps. But he doesn't lead.

But most mothers, traditionally, *do* lead. Without calling it leadership, mothers in most aspects of their work are leading. They are required to practise interactive thinking as well as promotional and structural thinking and often amass a wealth of management and leadership experience and information as a result. We need to recognize that fact.

When a friend and her husband were discussing his desire to give up work and her desire to work for pay outside the home, he said, 'Well, that would be fine except that Janice isn't qualified to do anything.' I had to laugh. She is a mother of five.

When the world recognizes the truth about mothering, it will give women the opportunity to choose mothering if they want to, and during their maternity leave, whether for weeks or years, stay updated and trained in their other profession or job. Women will put *Mother* prominently on their job application forms as professional experience.

Employers will be keen to recruit mothers because they will recognize the work as a valuable form of management and leadership training and experience.

We will also ensure that the job of mothering is well-paid. While mothers continue to face lower standards of living because they have become mothers, the leadership work of mothering will not be acknowledged. The challenge is to consider how to fund motherhood without drawing women away from public leadership. This is one of a vast number of critical social issues we need to take into thinking environments. We will need the best possible thinking conditions if good enough solutions are going to emerge.

I want to reiterate for women who do not have children that motherhood is by no means an essential requirement for thinking leadership. Whether or not to have children is an issue of choice, not of requirement. All women get practice in leadership simply by living in women's culture and by repudiating men's conditioning. It benefits all of us, though, to understand that mothering, a form of work done by nearly all women, is not a retreat from leadership.

As leaders, mothers can decide not to participate in sexism, not to torture their sons with male conditioning. In some parts of the world, we have begun to stop the torture of daughters with female conditioning: we now encourage girls to be assertive, scientific, athletic and political. We feel fairly comfortable teaching our girls to, in these positive ways, 'be more like boys'. But we still buy into sexism by inflicting tough-guy male conditioning on our sons. We need, instead, to encourage boys to be interactive, co-operative, flexible and connected; to, in these good ways, 'be more like girls'. This will be a decisive act of leadership and will change for the better the way people lead.

Just after the United States launched the first scud missile in Iraq my friend Cassie phoned me and said, 'At this morning's playgroup, Alison and Terry and I prevented violence thirteen times.

'I think we all felt like smacking the children. But we didn't.

'The most important thing I think we did was to put the children's attention on to what else was possible between them.

'We gave them choices that did not humiliate them; choices which kept their integrity intact. Basically we had to keep our nerve: we had to keep thinking. We could not just knock the children over and order them around.

'Now, I ask you, why can't they do this in Iraq? What is so different about it that they can't just do this? I know it is supposed to be much more complex. But is it?'

I think this question is worth contemplating.

Ironically, women's culture, including motherhood, seems to provide some of the best preparation for leadership. Men's culture does not. And yet men, brought up with male conditioning, make up more than 92 per cent of the leadership of the world. Could that in any way account for how dangerously close the world has got to self-destruction? We might want to consider making female culture the leadership training ground for both men and women. Soon.

PART 2

The Thinking Environment
in Practice

The greatest encouragement to think clearly will come from people who understand the nature of a thinking environment. It will take hold most successfully in people who understand sexist conditioning and its effects on thinking. In this section I present the ten components of a thinking environment in some detail and show through many stories the routes that will take us away from the traps of sexism, so that we can think afresh together.

I hope that if these stories remind you of issues and situations in your own life, they will serve as encouragement to master these components and treat yourself to a daily thinking partnership.

Take this incisive question with you in this section:

If you stopped holding back in your life right now, what would you do?

Imagine how you might take the lead in your relationships, your community, your office and even your country, as an expert in thinking environment principles and practice.

CHAPTER 6

Listening

Just to listen is an act of empowerment.

In your work with your thinking partner, the most important thing is to listen. Remember that listening is more than just not talking. It is as profound and delicate a process as entering a wood in the hope that life there will go on singing and scuttling and leaning towards the sun even with your arrival. Everything about you will have an effect on your partner's ability to keep thinking. You will want to be aware of the multitude of things you are doing and communicating while not becoming self-conscious. You will be balancing between awareness of yourself on the one hand and abandoned involvement in your partner's thinking on the other.

Words are not enough for this big job. Listening at this level uses your whole body and mind. Your body will be a barometer for your partner. You will want it to say, 'Everything is fine. I am interested. I think well of you. My only concern is that *you* should think of new ideas that will inspire and guide you to the life that is best for you and our world. I am not threatened by your words, nor am I jealous of your brilliance. We will often laugh and enjoy each other in this process, but I will not laugh at you. Here you can safely explore outrageous ideas; tell secrets, including those you haven't yet remembered; express strong feelings; and even be wrong. I am not judging you. I believe in you. I am keenly interested in what you are saying.' As you communicate this, your partner will start to relax and thinking can begin.

FACES
. . . .

Your face does most of the work of listening. It contains hundreds of muscles and almost all of them are in a state of constant communication with the world. Your face is probably saying more than you realize. It is probably also saying different things from the ones you think it's saying. By this stage in your life you have been through crises, you have felt sadness and fury, you have been frozen with terror, and day after day you have worried. Now, even as you rest, these things show. Brain scientists speculate that these events have made 'crevices' in your brain and that they determine the way we interpret events. They say that you will find yourself in the same circumstances over and over again until you consciously reassess these hurtful events and set up new kinds of behaviour, new crevices. This is still metaphor; we can't see these mental crevices.

But we can see the crevices in your face. They tell the stories of your pain and your joy, whether you want them to or not. Faces are fascinating that way, and growing older only makes us more fascinating and more beautiful. But these stories don't usually belong in a thinking session because they come from long ago and, though compelling, they are usually irrelevant and confusing obstacles in the path of your partner's thoughts.

And so they must be overriden by a face that says that this moment is fresh, and that this person you are listening to is unique. Your face can be taught to join your partner in the present and provide exactly the kind of backdrop that will encourage new ideas to form.

In fact, right now, examine your face. Hold it exactly where it is. What is it saying? Try not to move a single muscle in it and walk over to a mirror. It is saying what you thought it was saying? If you were sitting opposite that expression, what would you think its owner was thinking of you and what you had been saying? What effect would it have on what you said or thought next?

Now relax your face. Move it around. Smile. Frown. Wince. Wonder. Worry. Speculate. Condemn. Pretend. Your face is fabulous. It can say more, with less effort, than any other medium of communication. And it has an inestimable impact on the thinking processes of the people around you.

Your face can be a wondrous catalyst. But it can also be a minefield. In fact I hate to think how many wonderful ideas have exploded and disappeared as the person, caught in the wonderful abandon that characterizes exquisite thinking, tripped over the listener's old pain and set off the underlying bombs of reaction. While our partners are thinking, it is up to us, the listeners, to clear the minefields or at least to defuse the bombs. A thinking environment must be a reaction-free zone.

But that does not mean it is a response-free zone. On the contrary, our faces should respond unambiguously. They should communicate all kinds of things that will help the person keep thinking. Our facial responses should be positive, encouraging, curious, excited and always relaxed. In fact, I have seen people respond so well and so accurately that ideas seemed to form physically in the thinker's body and to be born with a serene, effortless exhilaration.

Notice the faces of your family. Notice how they look at you when they are listening to you. Family facial habits pass unaware through the generations. Let them stop with you.

Become aware of your face. And then get used to examining its expression from time to time. Until you become very good at keeping it in the present, it will have a tendency to slip back into the knots of your past and pollute the thinking session. You will not even know that this has happened and your partner will never know what ideas she has missed.

As you get more skilled at letting your face show the interest and ease that can keep your partner thinking, you will notice how gracefully ideas flow between you and how safe you become for each other.

Specifically, smile. Don't be shy about showing the delight your partner deserves. Now and then, perhaps more often than you feel comfortable doing, you can make a point of smiling, not for amusement but for encouragement. I am always surprised at how rarely people smile when they are listening to each other, particularly if they are listening to a difficult problem. We seem to feel obliged to join the person in their turmoil; we feel we can help if we writhe with them. But, in fact, we can be far more helpful by staying slightly dispassionate; by understanding and following what is said, interested in, but not overwhelmed by the story. We don't need to reflect back, with worried faces or moans, the pain the person is communicating. Instead, we need to reflect interest, permission to go on, the sense that there is a solution out there, and that we are fine. Too much empathy makes the thinker uneasy. She begins to worry about you.

Smile, but don't pretend. Better a worried face than a false pose.

Sincerity is one of the most important things in a thinking environment. Smile. But mean it.

Nod, too. But not excessively. The thinker needs to know that you are with her, that you understand. Nodding indicates that. But too much nodding, a head that bobs at every comma or each time the thinker looks up at you, is a signal to them to rush. The thinker will read it as, 'Please hurry and get to the end of this,' or, 'Yeah, yeah, I already know all this.' If it is your nervousness or your boredom at work, not your intelligence, don't do it.

Single sounds are also a signal of interest. 'Yes' and 'mmm' are the most familiar. But, again, don't overdo it. Too many of these reassuring mono-syllables communicate the same things as too many nods – 'I'm uneasy', 'Hurry up, I'm bored', and 'I'm trying to do this just right.' Well-placed monosyllabic sounds, however, can say 'Keep talking. I am with you.'

The key in all this is balance and appropriateness. You will be responding to what you hear, not giving responses based on pre-set instructions, or your own problems, history or agenda. In a way it is a relief to know that the best thing you can do is not be upset or try to solve the problem for the person. The best you can do is believe in them, encourage them, ask them to keep going, to say more, and then ask them questions that will take them past where they are stuck. It is fun. What works is shared intelligence, not shared agony.

SPACE

Notice where your body is in space. The space you set up between you and your partner is also a statement of interest and trust and will make a difference in what the person chooses to tell you and in how deeply and inventively she is able to explore the topic.

People who have been physically attacked, raped or molested, parti-cularly repeatedly in incestuous childhood experiences, require more space in order to be able to think with someone. People who have been spared this kind of abuse, on the other hand, often want to be very much closer when they are thinking about difficult and emotionally charged issues.

And some people require 2 feet of space in one situation and 10 feet in another. Often women can do their most advanced thinking with other women when they are fairly close, but would require three times the space when thinking about the same subject with a man. Men, on the other hand, because of the conditioning that keeps them physically terrified of other men and sexually obsessed with women, generally seem to require more space to think well than women. This of course changes according to the amount of male conditioning the man is struggling against.

Too much space, the kind that characterizes corporate board meetings, government committees, court rooms, classrooms and most conferences, puts a limit from the outset on the quality, range and freshness of ideas that can come out of the meeting. I have often been amused, when I am not being horrified, at these built-in obstacles in so many of the meetings which shape our lives. Peace summits, for example, are effectively sabotaged from the start by the accoutrements of diplomacy: distance, ritual, protocol and hierarchy. Real thinking has very little chance in that setting. And the proof is in the negative policies that emerge from such meetings. Most good ideas arise from a relaxed, fluid, spontaneous use of space.

It is best to ask. Find out how much space will work best for the person thinking and be prepared for that to change as trust builds and as more and more challenging subjects are discussed. Don't assume that you know.

EYES
. . . .

Go back to your face for a moment. Make eye contact with your thinking partner. Keep your eyes on her eyes. The thinker's eyes may go anywhere, but when she looks up at you, you have to be there. It is not good enough to come scurrying back. You have to be there already. There is nothing quite as disconcerting for someone venturing into new territory than having the other person 'walk away'. To keep reaching into unfamiliar thoughts and feelings, we need companionship and connection. Eyes say that best. As we talk, we need to have them on us every second.

There are two important exceptions to this rule. If you are blind, there will be other ways in which you can communicate this precise attention. Your partner will not be looking to your eyes for that reassurance. That 'visual' attention can be communicated through other facial muscles, through touch, through voice, and through body posture and tone.

And if you were both raised in a culture like the Aboriginal one, in which it is an insult to look directly at someone as you speak or listen, you will have come to understand, and use, other signals of attention.

But in sighted people or cultures, looking away can convey alarm, annoyance, timidity or lack of interest. And these can kill a thinking environment.

Keeping your eyes on the eyes of the thinker may be hard for you. Try it with someone today. Ask them to talk, and see how long you can keep up eye contact without looking away or looking down or wondering how you look. Notice what you find hard about it and talk about it with them when it is your turn. With practice you will come to enjoy paying attention this well. And you will quickly notice how much more easily people speak and think with you.

But, again, eye contact is not enough. The key ingredient of this process is *attention*. The more aware and interested and non-judgemental the attention, the more original the thinking will be. Even if you do not like the person or are furious with them – and this will happen at times in thinking sessions – keep your mind on what they are saying and on how close they are getting to their stated goal for the session. Your mind will be focusing on how they can come up with an idea that will work well for them and others. Stay intrigued by the new possibilities. You don't have to like your partners. You just have to be interested in their thinking.

UNTIL THEY HAVE SAID IT ALL

Much of the time listening well means listening exhaustively. Don't begin asking questions, removing obstacles for them, or giving advice (be very slow to do this in any case) until both of you are certain that the thinker has said everything she needs to say. You will do well to ask several times, 'Is there anything else?' And don't be surprised if you find that only with the third asking does she realize what she really needed to say all along. Often people edge up to the issue, testing their listeners for sincerity, endurance and interest, until they are sure they can trust them to help them think.

JUST LISTEN

Begin to look around you wherever you are and see what level of listening is commonplace in your world. Notice when the person speaking has to navigate through the rocks and storms and lulls she encounters in her listener. Sadly you may find that there is very little good listening going on in the world. And unfortunately, the more important it is for someone to listen well, the more poorly they seem to do it.

The more difficult or dangerous the problem, the more daring the thinking partner needs to be. Listening can be a great act of courage. We need to do this for each other many times a day.

'Sally is brilliant!' A colleague described her friend's girlfriend with this enthusiasm one day.

'What did Sally do?' I asked.

'She solved Yvonne's problem in less than five minutes.'

Later I asked Yvonne what Sally had said or done that had solved the problem so quickly. She didn't know exactly. She couldn't quite remember but said it had been amazing and that she thought Sally was the cleverest person she knew.

The next day I asked Yvonne again if she could remember what Sally had done.

'I don't know,' she said. 'That was what was so amazing. It didn't seem like anything. And I had been working that problem over the ages, getting nowhere. She just sat there and listened.'

Listening of this calibre is the foundation of a thinking environment. It is not all there is to to it. But it is the reason everything else works. And, once in a while, it is enough.

CHAPTER 7

Incisive Questions: The If Question

An incisive question can have a magical effect. My colleague Nancy says it is like play. As with many things, simple and wise, we often experience it unawarely when we are young. And, as with many things of childhood, it may also be a key to our power.

As a little girl I lived on the wide, dry plains near Texas. Most afternoons, however, I would go out of the back door and play outside in a make-believe deep Southern world of hawthorn trees, hedgerows, cow parsley and honeysuckle, all bordering an imaginary stream that ran to a make-believe river and wood just beyond. I remember sitting on the edge of the stream, which was actually a two-foot-wide ditch for the pipe Dad was laying at the time, and dangling my little feet in this gurgling playground for invisible birds. I could feel the stream's bank touch my toes with a squish and a bob, my skin actually grazing the clods and old grass roots that lay exposed after Dad's digging.

I think that may have been when I first started to understand the power and precision of incisive questions. Nothing as conscious as that was happening, of course. But day after day, I was entertaining new possibilities. In effect, I was asking myself, 'If this could be more to my liking, how would it be?' By asking that question, I was banishing the barriers between me and my Southern spring.

Incisive questions do this. They take away the barrier between where you are and where you want to be. They allow you to live on the other side of your own limitations long enough to know that you can eventually get there in reality.

Most of us live indoors, on the safe, familiar side of our lives. This is true whether we are talking about big dreams for ourselves and our world or about the little dilemmas that throttle our ordinary days. Incisive questions sweep away the limits that bind us to the same old way of doing things. They extend our current territory and open up with a whoosh the unexplored terrain we have barely been able to acknowledge in ourselves. And, like my stepping outside to play, they make the new view easy. In a flash it is before us.

For example, think, for a moment, about what is holding you back in your life right now, the assumption or circumstance that is a barrier for you. What if it weren't there? If this barrier were not part of your thinking any longer, how would things be different for you?

Sometimes you have to go further, to explore the barriers in layers to find the one at the core. For example, if you have identified the thing holding you back as your boss, you may find it is actually your fear of being your real self with your boss that lies beneath that barrier. (However, you may not; there are some truly horrible bosses out there.) But if you do, you may then find that beneath that barrier is an excessive need for other people's approval. In that case, the core incisive question might be, 'If you could believe that it is best to be your *real* self regardless of what others think of you, what would you change immediately?'

Ask a question like that and, for a moment, the barrier vanishes. You can then think in new ways. This is one definition of power: the ability to let go of the assumptions and to think without the givens, no longer to think as a victim.

KATE
. . . .

Kate had a specific problem about work.

'I need to get a proper job', she said, 'and I don't know which one to choose from the ones I've been offered. I want to enjoy my job and advance in it, and have some authority. I am good at a lot of things and I could train quickly. The main thing I want is autonomy and good pay. My real problem is that I need to make enough money to pay my debts and help my mother out. That's why I need a proper job. Mother says I just have to keep looking and I'll find one.'

'What have you looked at so far?' Jessica, her thinking partner, asked.

'Well, I am trying to decide between being a researcher, a bank clerk, a volunteer co-ordinator, an insurance clerk, or running a nursery. They all pay quite well.'

'What do you *want* to do?'

'That isn't the point,' Kate said.

'What *is* the point?'

'That I want to make the best choice. I want to work out which of these proper jobs will give me the most autonomy and enjoyment. And I don't know how to do that.'

Now, what would you have asked Kate next? What was the assumption in her way? What question(s) would have removed that barrier/ assumption so that she could see the possibilities open to her?

Her partner was exactly right. 'If you did not have to get a proper job, what would you want to do?' Jessica said.

It would have been fruitless for Jessica to have asked Kate, for example, about the good and bad points of her five proper job options and it would have been pointless to keep asking her what she really wanted in general. It was the 'proper' job assumption that was dictating everything. It had to be removed so that she could think freely about this problem. Kate looked incredulous.

'But that's not possible. Everyone says that you can earn steady money only from a proper job and that anything else is too risky and foolish. Everyone.'

'But if they were wrong and you could meet your financial needs by not doing a proper job, what would you do?'

'If I didn't have to get a proper job?' Kate asked, as if she had just heard the question for the first time. 'Well, now, that's an amazing question. Hmmm. If I didn't have to get a proper job . . . And still earn enough money? Amazing. Well, under those highly unrealistic circumstances, I know exactly what I would do. I'd turn my garage into a children's theatre and help ten-year-olds put on musical plays.'

'And if you assumed people would want to pay you to do this, how would you get started?'

She laughed. 'I'd get local businesses and parent teacher associations and the emergency services and every middle-class parent working outside the home to contribute money as a way of keeping children happy and safe after school and on Saturdays.'

'And what would be your very first step in doing this?' Jessica asked.

Without hesitation Kate said, 'I'd phone my friend Jana. I think she knows someone in every one of those groups. And she has a ten-year-old daughter who comes home alone after school'.

That is how the Children's Neighbourhood Lyric Theatre began. It is still going and has moved out of a garage without losing its imaginative core. Ironically, Kate effectively created a proper job for herself. She now earns her living as the director of the theatre.

Incisive questions open doors and it is often as swift, direct, and smooth as Jessica and Kate's experience. It is like a child's imaginary play, but with one difference: it is not a fantasy. It derives from our real situation, needs and desires and then goes far beyond them. The question recognizes the barrier of the limiting assumption in our way and removes it.

ALICE
. . . .

Alice was despondent. She thought it must be because she was getting old – she was forty-nine. She told Fran that she did not like her work any more even though she was director of one of the city's biggest social work agencies and even though she created and ran her own projects. She had always liked work and gained energy from it. But now she was tired. And the work she was doing reflected her fatigue – it was lusterless, often late, incomplete and sometimes inconclusive.

'I don't know what's wrong. I go into my office and I feel like giving up. The project I was so enthusiastic about seems to have got dull and distant. Nobody in the government wants to think about it. I'm interested in teenage pregnancies but this is not a big election issue so other things demand my attention. I have piles of interviews to complete on my desk, letters and masses of things to sign and review. I get to my desk each morning and never even finish the things my boss thinks are urgent. The teenage pregnancy issue that stays buried.

'My boss breaks every appointment I make with him. I tell him not to do this, but I have not been able to get him to sit down and talk to me for the past three months. He nearly always cancels whatever I arrange.'

Fran listened. Then, when Alice had finished and clearly had no more to say, Fran said, 'If you were to go to the office tomorrow, bouncy and powerful, what would be different about work?'

Alice smiled, then burst out laughing. 'Bouncy and powerful! How marvellous. Now that is a different point of view. If I were bouncy and powerful, well, now, I would be quite a different person from the one you see today. I would change some things, all right. I would set up a thinking partnership with one of the women near me for a start. Then I would delegate all the clerical details of my work to a secretary and put off the interviews. I would begin this big teenage pregnancy project immediately and not wait until all that administrative work was done. And I would make an appointment with the boss that he couldn't break. I don't know how, but I would this time.'

Alice looked like a different person. She had burst into life; she had changed from a victim to a powerful woman. The difference radiated out of her and changed her face and her posture.

SONYA

A similar change happened for Sonya. Aged sixteen, Sonya told her young women's group that a boy doing research in their school library had motioned to her to come over to his desk. Thinking he wanted help with a reference, she walked across to him. When she leaned over his shoulder to look at his text, he pulled his penis out of his trousers and said, 'Come and get it, pretty girl.'

She was terrified. She walked away trembling from head to toe. She said he was in the library the next day. She stayed clear of him, but when the other people had left the room, he stood up and, waving his penis at her, said, 'What are you scared of, bitch?'

She ran out of the library and into the headmaster's office. He calmed her down and found out what had happened. But he said there was very little he could do because it was her word against the boy's word. If they caught the boy at it, that would be different. But the possibility of false accusations was dangerous both to her and to the school. He also said that he would need to be sure she hadn't provoked the boy to do it in the first place. She left his office numb and confused.

'I am too scared to go back into that library,' she said to the young women. 'But it is my after-school job and I have to.'

'If you weren't afraid of him, what would you do?' Sarah asked her.

'But I *am* afraid!' Sonya said.

'Of course you are; anyone would be. It's disgusting what he is doing. But just consider it for a minute. Right now he isn't here and cannot hurt you, right? So try to imagine that you are not scared of him, that he is scared of you, instead. What would you do?'

'That'd be the day. He is six foot two.'

'True. But he isn't here at the moment, is he? So what would you do if you weren't scared?'

'Scream like hell.'

'Good . . .' Sarah said.

'No, actually, what I'd really do,' Sonya blurted out, 'if I weren't so scared, is say in a confident voice that the next time I see him, "Jeremy, would you PLEASE put your penis back into your trousers and stop calling me pretty girl. IMMEDIATELY!"'

Everyone laughed. It was the kind of laughter that releases fear.

'Good!' Sarah collected herself enough to say. 'So tell us again and notice how powerful you are.'

She did. They all laughed again. And as she did it for the third time, she began to feel a bit less flushed and quivery at the thought.

'The thing is, though,' she paused, 'I really do have to do this. Really. I don't know if I can.'

'What might stop you?' Sarah asked.

'Well, I wouldn't know what to do next.'

'And if you weren't confused afterwards, what would you do?'

'I'd leave the library and . . .'

'And?'

'And all of you would be waiting for me and we would celebrate!'

And that is exactly what happened. A week later Sarah told me that the group had met Sonya at the school before she went into the library that day and had had her practise the scenario one more time. Then, within the hour, Sonya had come out of the library, successful, had found the group waiting for her in the hall, and they had cheered and hugged each other and talked about it over and over again.

Notice how sensitive Sarah had been during that thinking time for Sonya. She did not do the things people usually feel compelled to do. She did not give advice. She did not commiserate. She did not tell Sonya about her own experiences of sexual harassment. She did not change the subject. She did not reassure her that the boy would not do it again. She did not ask Sonya if she had done something to provoke him, implying that it was Sonya's fault. And she did not get hopeless and say something like, 'Well, I don't know what I would do either. I'd be scared to death.'

People think such responses help others. But they rarely do. What helps is listening and asking incisive questions that get the thinker to go beyond her self-enforced limitations and come up with a new idea that only she could have thought of.

A friend who calls this process 'magic' says that asking incisive questions is like two people walking together, parallel, down one person's path. On your own path, you have grown used to detouring or turning back when you come upon the old blocks in your way. In fact, you turn away automatically, not even seeing the barriers as barriers. You have encountered them for so many years that they seem like the road itself. And you fail each time to get to your destination and are frustrated or depressed without understanding why or what to do.

But your partner has not been on this road before and so she sees the barriers for what they are. She also sees a path stretching dependably ahead beyond the barriers and so she can lift them out of your way. Suddenly a whole new picture opens up before you, a streamlined path that you wonder how you ever missed. Her questions cleared the way.

MARY

Mary held an elected office and voted on national legislation nearly every week. She was also one of four women who met once a month as a women's thinking group. They often had to meet in hotel conference rooms over lunch near the houses of government so that Mary could get maximum time with the group and still rush back to be present for the vote.

At one meeting Mary was late and had only ten minutes for her thinking session while she ate her sandwich. I watched an impressively efficient thinking partnership at work that day. Mary spoke in despairing circles about the pressure in electoral government to conform and about her confused values. When she had talked enough, her thinking partner asked her, 'What is the thing you want most to achieve before you retire from politics?'

Mary did not hesitate. 'I want to have helped make women's lives better.'

'And if you were to keep women's lives in the forefront of your legislative work, what would you do today?'

Again, Mary said without difficulty, 'I would vote against the changes in today's bill because they remove women's benefits. And then I would reintroduce the women's clause and make it even stronger.'

'Good,' her partner said. 'Now you must go. We will be cheering you on from here!'

It had been a bit breathless, but it had worked. Most startling was the fact that Mary's despair had lifted and, in less than ten minutes, she was up and running with renewed resolve.

'If' questions are often incisive because 'if' is a magic wand. 'If' changes one situation into another. And when we use it accurately, removing the limiting assumption and leaving behind open space, options pour in.

But 'if' questions are not the only incisive questions. A question is incisive when it forces out the conditioning, the barrier, the unworkable assumption. And the shape of the question can vary.

MINA
. . . .

Mina said she wished she could have a six-hour break from the endless demands of her job and her family.

'Just six hours,' she said.

'What would it take for you to get that?' her friend asked.

That was an incisive question. Her friend had put the power back in Mina's hands. She hadn't asked, 'Why can't you get that kind of time?' or 'What makes you think anyone ever gets that kind of time?' or 'Who else in your family works like this?' or 'Are you trying to kill yourself or something?'

'What would it take for you to get that?' she asked.

'Permission,' Mina said.

'From whom?'

'Myself.'

'Do it.'

'Do it?'

'Yes. Do it. Give yourself permission right now.'

'Really?'

'Yep.'

'Just like that?'

'Yes. Why not?'

'Okay . . . Well, I hereby give myself permission to take six whole hours just for me.'

'Good,' her friend said. 'Now what will you do with the time?'

'I don't know, but I know I want to do only *gorgeous* things. I think I'll ask myself all day, "What is the next gorgeous thing I can do?"'

That was like an incisive question on tap. All day long it removed any guilt barriers that might have blocked her ideas of how to keep the six hours just for herself.

That whole exchange took only a few minutes, but it made a great difference in how Mina spent her time and in the effect that time had on the rest of her week.

Looking for the barrier as you listen, and removing it with a question, can make streams run under wiggly toes in the middle of the plains.

CHAPTER 8

Incisive Questions:
What Do You Really Want?

'What do you really want?' is nearly always the right question. More often than not, this is the question that rolls the barriers away. In fact, it is so often the right question that asking it can sometimes seem far too easy. It is often the perfect question not because the only thing that matters in the world is what we want. It is more a reflection of how very, very little we *know* about what we want and how seldom we factor it into our thinking.

The chances are that you have made nearly every decision today without considering that question. Sexist conditioning, for both men and women, convinces us that what we want is irrelevant, that we are here to do what is expected of us and that to ask the question is an act of selfishness. From the most trivial things to matters of national importance, people often forget to ask the question before they make a decision.

The question takes on new dimensions as women take more leadership in a male-dominated world. There we run into what I call the power-for-silence bargain: if we agree to be silent, men grant us power. True, we are granted new platforms and constituencies to address, and we're given the media on a silver platter for a while, but we cannot talk about the sensitive things, the things that brought us to the attention of the establishment in the first place. Having alarmed the powers that be by speaking out on specific issues, they decide to give us a little taste of power in exchange for our silence.

In the Introduction I said that women must begin to recognize when our oppression looks and feels like freedom. The power-for-silence bargain is one example of this insidious phenomenon. When we are offered a place inside the power structure, we can easily feel relieved and victorious. But relief is not the same thing as well-being, it is only a temporary cessation of pain. And if our entrance fee to the halls of power has been the relinquishing of our voice, the packing away of our values, we soon find that we are actually more confined and in more pain than before. Not only do we not have real power; we now have no platform from which to protest our oppression, either. That is how the controlling forces want it – they can get rid of us while looking supportive. This is another example of how men remain the architects of women's liberation.

We can avoid the power-for-silence bargain in several ways. One is to master the art of finding out what we *really* want and to base our decisions on the true answer. Then, with our eyes wide open and our true goals as our guide, we can enter the power structure and not be disempowered in the process. It is when we don't know what we really want, when we don't know what our *real* goals are, that we are vulnerable to the seduction of silence, to oppression that looks and feels like freedom.

But to do this we have to know our real selves well. We have to find out what we truly do want and then think with someone about how to achieve it. I have watched women struggle with this challenge and succeed, women at different levels of decision-making, including a woman of significant power in the non-partisan women's movement of a large city. 'Anne virtually runs this city,' a mutual colleague of ours said to me one day. 'That's not true, of course. No woman runs this city or any other city for that matter. But Anne's influence is phenomenal.'

But when Anne came to me to discuss her next steps, the road did not look that clear. Yes, she had the influence; and yes, she was being offered opportunities in politics and public life. But she was deeply troubled. She did not know what to do. So we went back to the basic question. I asked her to tell me her goals and dreams for her work. 'What do you really want, Anne?' I asked her and then listened for a long time.

'I want the power, the chance to make changes in this country; I want a forum for my ideas in government; I want to do more and more of what I have done for the past ten years, but I don't want to get cut off from the women I have worked with all this time. I don't know whether politics is the way to do this. I am afraid that if I do seek an elected position, I will get lost in the pleasing that politicians have to do to stay elected. I have watched so many people virtually disappear as soon as they reach office; they start talking only about soft, safe issues and nothing changes.'

We talked for a while about the power-for-silence bargain and about the temptation to seem to gain power while losing power in the process. Again I asked her, 'What do you really want?'

This time she was more concise. 'I want to be a voice for women for the rest of my life.'

And so I asked her, 'If you could trust yourself to keep your voice once you were in the halls of power, what would your course be?'

She paused. 'I would have to be willing to be kicked out.'

She went on, 'I would have to remember that my purpose for being there was to be heard, not to be re-elected. That would be hard.'

After much struggle with this, Anne decided to stand for office. Her almost daily challenge then was to stay alert to the signals of seduction, the sounds of oppression masquerading as freedom, the relief that comes with publicity and applause, and, as she put it, to keep her mind focused ahead on her eightieth birthday when she hopes to say that she did what she wanted to do – she spent her life being a voice for women.

The question 'What do you really want?' is important in situations as public as this one was in Anne's life. But it is just as important in private decisions. They eventually add up to the measure of our life and need just as much care and integrity as the public ones.

At an AIDS conference in England Amanda Heggs, a woman from Denmark who has HIV, spoke about her experience as a woman with the virus. A number of things she said were about sexism and the way it keeps us from knowing what we want, even from valuing our own lives.

She was telling the story of how she became infected, saying that her lover had been travelling abroad, and that about a year after his return, they had both become ill. She found out later that he had known all along that he was HIV positive but had not told her and had subsequently infected her. He hadn't told her because he didn't like using condoms and because he was afraid of losing his masculinity if he couldn't prove it by making children.

She said, 'It's too simplistic to say that the sole reason for my being infected was male chauvinism. I was infected also because I was never taught that it is legitimate to work out what I want and to put demands on my partner. Neither was I brought up to learn that my own life was also worth protecting, and that it was my responsibility.'

Female conditioning keeps women miles away from knowing what we really want. And male conditioning keeps men from asking us. It stops men considering what impact their actions will have on the lives of women. It stops men thinking about a woman's life except as it directly affects theirs. Inside male conditioning men are surprised to hear this because they are not wilfully ignoring women's lives and concerns and points of view. It just doesn't occur to them to think about them. It does not enter their thoughts that women are at least as embroiled, as stimulated, as troubled, as ambitious, as concerned, as perplexed as they are.

Oppression makes us invisible to men and to ourselves. But the question 'What do you really want?' can help us reappear, take up space and be a force to be reckoned with. We can realize that, although we did not initiate our own feelings of non-existence, we are nevertheless responsible for removing them.

If you were assigned the task of disempowering a group of people so that they would obey you even to their own detriment and if you were allowed only one weapon to effect such a devastating disability, what would you use? Convincing them that they must never ask the question 'What do I really want?' would probably do it.

The conditioning of women and men is exactly this kind of disempowering weapon. Women's conditioning is explicit about this. Women are to serve others. Particularly, men. Then, children. Then, friends. Then, organizations. Increasingly, our employers. Then our countries. Rarely ever, ourselves. Our thinking capacity is disabled because we cannot think about the question 'What do you really want?' Even our highly encouraged interactive thinking skills can grow blunt because we use them for martyrdom instead of empowerment.

When we cannot ask ourselves the question about our own lives, we cannot ask it about the lives of women in general. Sometimes we find ourselves embarrassed to talk publicly about women's needs. At work, for example, we are often afraid to make companies address issues such as paid childcare, single parent needs, health information, and flexitime. We are much, much more comfortable ignoring women's issues and talking about men's perception of what is needed. We demean women's needs in proportion to the amount we demean our own needs.

We can think of only a narrow range of ideas to solve a problem because we factor ourselves out of the equation, and when we do, we factor out all women and their particular needs.

This may account for women's willingness to support political manifestoes in which women's needs are hardly mentioned and to support a government in which women are still a thin minority of the power. It can account for the disturbing enthusiasm many women have for female heads of state who never mention (or appoint) women. Our conditioning to put ourselves last individually can perpetuate the state of political disempowerment globally.

I invited a new colleague of mine to attend a workshop I am presenting called 'Woman Rest: A Gathering of Mothers to Think About Themselves.' I told her that the motto for this workshop was 'A time to do nothing and rest afterwards.' She told me the next day that she thought all night about the title and realized with a crash that she virtually never thinks about herself, about what she might want. She said, 'I am always doing things for other people and that is absolutely the only way I can be happy.'

The very tricky thing about beginning to ask the question 'What do I really want?' is that by now we are so practised at *not* thinking about ourselves, and so convinced at an emotional level that *our worth as women actually derives from putting ourselves last*, that we experience emotional and physical discomfort at the thought of asking the question. That unease confuses us, and we back off from asking, assuming that there is something wrong with the question, rather than with our discomfort.

One of the most intelligent things we can do is make this question our starting point for any dicussion, problem-solving, decision, negotiation or policy. Once you have worked out what you really want, and the others in the discussion have worked out what they each really want, you can think together about a stunning new idea that will provide *all* of you with what you want. If not all of you are being considered, if *your* needs are not part of the discussion, whatever happens will be only partially right; it will not work well enough.

You may insist that you are happy only when you are considering others' needs, not your own (i.e. that you can't stand the discomfort of going against your conditioning). But, if you persist in living this way, you will become less and less happy. You will fill huge pools of yourself with resentment. You will grow bitter, unengaging, angry with others.

Over time, your long neglected needs will begin to seep through the structures of your life until your world, large or small, first hears them, then smells them, digs trenches for them, wades through them, and finally drowns in it. In the long run, leaving yourself out of the equation is the most selfish thing you can do.

It is no accident that mental institutions for people over fifty-five are dominated by women. Unexpressed needs lead eventually to severe depression, repressed rage, disorientation, illness, and finally death.

I've known women who I am sure died of sexism. The death certificate said 'aneurism' or 'stroke' or 'cancer'. But I wonder . . . 'Poisoning' would be more like it – 'death by the highly toxic effect of suppressed needs.'

Sometimes what we call mental collapse in women is actually a collapse of their iron will to ignore themselves. It is a kind of explosion of needs all at once. It is almost a perverse act of liberation. I have heard women say, 'I can't stand this any more. I don't know who I am, where I am going, why I do what I do. Even though I've seemed happy, I've been miserable for most of my life.' As painful as it is to hear women reach this point of despair, it can also be strangely heartening. It can be heard as a refusal to go on ignoring themselves. But it is a tragic way for them to do it. It is a grim outcome of the bogus satisfaction of self-sacrifice.

At the age of seventy-six Elizabeth, having seen psychiatrists off and on for a year, turned to her middle-aged son and said, 'I think I have a problem now. I don't like my life and I don't know what to do.'

In his forty-five years Alex had never heard his mother say anything so direct about her feelings. Always controlled, even sometimes severe, she had raised four children, all infants during the war, seen to the care of her husband who scolded her even when he said good morning and who only rarely put down his book or paper to converse but whom she was quick to defend as a good husband and dependable provider. She had cooked four meals a day for fifty years.

She had organized events at her church, and looked after many neighbours and relations who were getting on in years. She remembered every grandchild's birthday and stoically agreed to be celebrated on her own. She wasted not one penny on heat or clothing or travel. She had not cried since her brother died at sea when she was twelve. And for this she had been called brave.

Alex asked her tenderly, 'What do you *want* to do, Mother?'

87

'I just want to die. I just want to live somewhere else.'

'Where do you want to go?' Alex asked.'

'Anywhere. Anywhere but here.'

'If you could leave, where would you go right now?'

'I'd go downstairs . . .'

With uncharacteristic boldness Elizabeth looked at him, stood up, and walked down the stairs.

She walked over to the sitting area and sat in her customary chair across from Julian's customary chair. Julian did not look up from his book.

'Julian,' Elizabeth said.

'What?' he grunted.

'I can't go on like this. I do not like my life, and I want to leave.'

'What did you say?' He looked up.

'I can't go on like this. I do not like my life, and I want to leave.'

'That is rubbish', he shouted, 'absolute rubbish! Of course you like your life. You have everything you need and you are perfectly happy. Now we won't speak of this again.' He picked up his book, squared his shoulders and settled back into his chair.

She looked away from him and over to the fireplace. Her eyes widened and her back sagged into the chair. 'Yes,' she whispered slowly to herself, 'yes, that is right, isn't it; yes, happiness, husband, hearth and home, yes.'

She rarely spoke after that. Weeks went by. She did nothing. She cooked nothing. She said nothing. She sat in her chair in front of the fire.

When she eventually accepted a room in the mental hospital nearby and was told that she would have to be there at least six months, she began to talk again. She played Scrabble again and offered to lay the table for tea and sometimes for dinner. She shared a room with six other people and spoke kindly of all but one of them.

When I visited her, I sensed that she had found this to be a way to leave her husband and her home with permission. Somehow in this sad environment she seemed almost happy. She had found what was for her a socially acceptable way to release herself from her prison of self-sacrifice and denial. Here she was expressing her needs and people were listening.

Every time she went back home, she had a relapse and became virtually autistic again. In the hospital she gradually emerged to speak and smile occasionally and to welcome visitors.

Three years later, in a nursing home, she recently sent a birthday card to her husband (he is in a nursing home 60 miles away), signed with an expression of private affection between them from fifty-three years ago. And, no, she doesn't want to see him. 'But wish him well, please,' she said to Alex.

This is the story of one person's life. But I see it also as an analogy for the life of our society's structures and systems. Along the way, particularly in the early years of its construction, we did not as a society of women ask what *we* really wanted, and we did not develop a thinking environment in which to consider this question. We just went along with the loudest, most threatening voices, and the structures grew.

And now we plod on through the structures of government, of business, and of society that were formed for us, trying to believe in them, wondering why they injure, but determinedly not complaining. We prop them up with denial and patriotism. We hardly notice that the world shouts at us, 'Of course these are the best systems in the world. You are very fortunate. You love them and we will not speak of this again.'

And we are dying inside them. Inside these unconsidered systems our choices are few. So we must speak up. And we must think beyond the barriers of custom and rhetoric. Way, way beyond them.

But we must start now, while we still can, with the question, 'What do I really want?' It may take us a long time to answer it. But we can be patient with ourselves and each other. Old habits don't yield overnight. And the implications of answering the question are not insignificant. Changes will occur, and we have to think through those changes.

This question makes you face your real excellence. Tara, a long-time manager of a company, ran up against this challenge when she and Carl, her husband, also a manager, decided to leave the company.

The farewell dinner for employees and board members was a week away. Tara phoned her friend Lela to think about how she would get through the experience without crying.

'Sam is eliminating my position as soon as we leave. As director, he has never seen the value of what I have done, not even right at the beginning when what I did brought in customers and profits that probably saved the company. I know it is sexism. But there is something else. I hate it, but I don't know what it is.'

Lela kept listening.

'At the dinner I want to criticize everyone, especially Sam, for his unawareness. But I know that is not appropriate. I haven't done it to his face in twenty years. So I suppose I won't do it now. Not there, anyway. It wouldn't change anything. And I wouldn't want to embarrass Carl.

'This dinner is important to Carl. He is going to make a speech and probably everyone will cry and, as always, he will be wonderful. Maybe I should just not speak.'

Lela kept listening.

'I've never spoken at an event there. Never. I wouldn't have any idea what to say. I would be terrified. Carl's speech will be fabulous.'

'What do you want to do, Tara?' Lela asked.

'Oh, I don't know. I just want to survive the damn thing.'

'Well, besides that, what do you want?'

Tara thought for a minute. 'I'd really like to speak. Women hardly ever do that there. Even the assistant directors and heads of department just sit back and the men do the public speaking at things like this. It is practically prehistoric. But I don't know what I'd say.'

Tara paused a while, and looking into her eyes, Lela could see the wonderful dance that goes on when someone is considering a new possibility.

'What are you thinking?' she asked.

'That I might be really, really good at that,' Tara said, hardly above a whisper.

'Yes?' Lela encouraged her.

'What if I were good?' Tara considered.

'What if you were?' Lela asked.

'God, I don't know. I wonder what I would talk about.'

'Well, what do you *want* to talk about?' Lela asked.

'I don't know. What do I *want* to talk about?' Tara mused. 'What do I want to talk about?'

'In fact, if you were going to talk so that you would be seen as dignified, not as a fool, and so that everyone would be moved, what would you want to say?'

And Tara began to think. She knew what she wanted to say.

The next day she rang Lela again and read her the speech she had written. It was excellent. Lela cried. And Tara said, 'I have to tell you what happened to me as I was writing this. I realized that for twenty years I have held back in the company because I did not want to outshine Carl. I can think of so many times when I actually thought in a flash that,

90

if I did such and such, Carl might not look so good. Sam got away with murder because of this. What I really want is to shine. But how can I agree to put Carl in my shadow?'

'Carl can shine, too,' Lela said. Simple. The theory of limited resources applies to oil and trees and water, but not to things like excellence, ideas or love.

Tara gave a wonderful speech, thanking the company for its values in achieving a long list of things that in fact made up her twenty-year contribution to the company. And she encouraged the company to go all the way with its vision, not to sit on the talents of women or on the hearts of men. Many people cried. They cried after Carl's speech, too. No shadows. Just sun.

So now, it is your turn. Take the question 'What do you really want?' into your life. Get used to it. Notice the need for it a hundred times a day. Practise asking it, even when you are too scared to hear its answers and follow its implications. Eventually you will count on it as a way back to yourself and as an incisive tool for the life and leadership you want.

You will see its political implications, too. It has to be the starting point for the big policies and even the infrastructures of our economy, social systems and global interactions if we are ever going to have the world we envision. Its absence is probably one reason why our political parties offer us few real choices, our corporations require exploitation, and our productivity seems to have to destroy the environment.

We have to stop in the middle of everything and ask the question. No matter how many horns screech at us, no matter how many commuters shout at us, no matter how many green lights we miss, we must stop and ask. It is possible to find out where we are going and decide whether that is what we want. If it isn't, it is probably not too late to change direction.

And remember, if what you want seems sure to destroy everything you have built, you can think systematically about that, too. Everything that seems to be a problem can be solved with enough thinking time and a thinking environment. Nothing is too hard for us when we treat each other this well.

So.

When it comes to your power, how far do you *want* to go?

CHAPTER 9

Incisive Questions:
What Do You Really Think?

The one topic we could never successfully discuss in my family was the Vietnam War. Other taboo subjects we could manage. Even homosexuality in the Church we could talk about and still kiss each other goodnight at the end. Coolly. But usually with a smile and a pat, reassuring ourselves that by morning everything would be back to normal.

In fact, in my family I was encouraged to talk generally. Mother listened tirelessly to virtually everything I said from the first minute I said anything, which Dad claimed was as soon as I was born. (That was about as vicious as the jokes got in my family.)

Mother's child-rearing philosophy included establishing her children's dignity and self-respect by listening to them. She extended this principle to children other than her own as well. I remember every Saturday afternoon when my sister and her friend Anne returned from the cinema, Mother sat at that kitchen table with them and listened to Anne retell the plot of the film, blow by blow, boring detail by boring detail, until I thought her ears would drop off.

When I grew up, and asked her how she ever stood the tedium, she said, 'It wasn't tedious at all. I knew that if I listened long enough to Anne, she would one day turn out to be interesting.' I have to hand it to Mother. Anne is now one of the most interesting storytellers I know.

As long as we stayed on subjects that did not stir her disapproval, Mother listened and listened. It was from her that I learned the beginnings of a thinking environment. It was from Dad that I learned to speak out.

But the Vietnam War was a different matter. Every discussion of this event, as it was called, was explosive. One reason for this was that anything the US military did was, in my parents' mind, a good thing to do. This belief was particularly rooted in the embers of Second World War patriotism and particularly in the US determination to avoid the 'Chamberlain appeasement trap'. After war, nations spend a long, long time confusing the present with the past.

But it did not go unnoticed by me, even then when I had a political IQ of about nil, that our small town population doubled in size and so did many incomes, including my father's when, after Dad's lobbying, the Defence Department reactivated the airforce base there.

Also, for generations, everyone in my parents' families had believed in what was called a strong defence. Since 1776, when we defeated the British, it had been accepted that we would have a strong military force to take care of encroaching nations. Additionally, my father, as a Southerner, did not want to be defeated ever again. That was another war that made the present and the past vaguely indistinguishable.

But the real reason for the explosions about Vietnam was that my twin brother was fighting there. He was flying in and out of Da Nang in a monster C141 transport plane, a plane big enough to carry many tanks and many weapons and many, many dead bodies. How could I question the morality of something when any minute my brother might give his life for it?

So we either didn't bring up the subject, or we screamed at each other. And, as you know, too much dissension seemed to cause my mother to stop breathing. So I usually kept quiet. I saw discussion of the Vietnam War as a serious health and safety risk in those days.

Time went on. More and more I wanted to understand what all the protest marches were about and why ending the war wouldn't be safer for Bill than fighting on. But I didn't talk about it much. I tried to put it out of my mind. When there is no thinking environment, there is not much thinking. And I tried to console myself with Dad's theory that the real enemies were the Russian Communists who were plotting to take over our great country, and would very likely land on the East Coast and reach our little town 2000 miles away within days of taking New York, if we did not hold them back in South-East Asia. I kept trying to believe that all those dominoes could fall, and at the same time prayed that Bill's plane would make it into the air before the enemy rockets hit the fuel tanks around him.

During this period I got a job teaching English at a Quaker school in Maryland. I did not know this when I accepted the job, but Quakers were as fervently against that war as my father was for it. These Quakers were also very different from my childhood Southern Methodist community. It was 1968 and all the boys there had long hair; all the teachers drove Volkswagen beetles; all the women wore long cotton skirts and old sweaters; and they met every morning for 15 minutes in a cold building called the Barn just to be quiet together. That was called meeting for worship.

I, on the other hand, arrived wearing expensive woollen suits with fashionably short hems and high-heeled shoes, driving a four-door Chevrolet, hailing from a strict tradition of boys with crew cuts, and trained from boarding school in the art of talking to prevent the undesirable event of silence.

I still think it was a great act of faith that they took me on at all.

One day we met in the Barn, not for silence this time, but for something different. It was called a town meeting. There the whole school discussed issues together, particularly issues that people felt strongly about. The format was simple. Anyone could talk and everyone had to listen. It went on as long as it needed to. Somehow the clerk of the meeting, the person in charge, would know when that was. It was all pretty vague but it seemed to work. The meetings did end and people always accepted it when they did.

What I noticed about these town meetings was that it really was all right for anyone to say anything and people really did listen. They did not interrupt or shout at each other or contradict the person speaking. They listened, and when one person had finished, the next person spoke. This went on until that mysterious thing happened with the clerk and it was over.

One day I stood up and spoke. That day people had been talking about the war. Everyone was saying that it should stop, that it was not a war we should be fighting and that the domino theory was wrong. I was furious.

I stood up and said I thought the war was the only way to keep our national freedom. And I sat down. The next person spoke, saying more about why the US should leave Vietnam.

Afterwards I noticed that nobody hated me.

Week after week we had town meetings on this issue. And week after week I stood up and said the same thing. And week after week nobody hated me. They just kept listening and stating their point of view.

Nixon had been elected on a strong pro-war platform. I was the only one at the school who watched his inauguration. Bill flew his tenth mission to Da Nang and carried back the full body bags to New Jersey. Later the press reported the My Lai massacre of babies and women by US soldiers.

After one of the town meetings I walked across the campus to my colleague Peter's office, talking to him about the war. Like the other faculty members, he listened to me and usually replied firmly but calmly. He was also good at asking questions.

We sat down in his office among piles of papers and magazines and thousands of books, and he listened to me say again that, though the war was terrible, it was better than the possibility of Russia invading our country which was sure to happen if we pulled out of Vietnam. Then, wanting to know what I thought, he asked, 'When the Russians arrive in New York, what exactly do you think they will do with it?'

Some moments change your life. This was one of them for me. I had no idea what the Russians would do with New York. And what they were going to do with my little home town 2000 miles away a few days later was even more of a mystery.

But for the first time I was having to work out what *I* really thought. The need to be right, or to defend myself or my brother, or to be sure that my mother was still breathing, was not there. The man simply wanted to know what I thought. I had to think about that, I wasn't sure.

I remember feeling the way I had ten years before, the very first time I skated on ice. I couldn't work out to get both my legs to go forward at the same time and not slip sideways. But Peter was in no hurry, and was even happy for me to take days to answer the question if I needed to.

The fact that I, like so many other Americans, eventually saw fallacies in our beliefs about that war was less important for me than the experience of his implied incisive question 'What do you really think?', and the right environment in which to consider it.

Like asking 'What do you really want?', the question 'What do you really think?' is dangerous. If asked in a thinking environment, it will almost certainly lead to upheaval. Sometimes only this question can succeed in removing barriers for people, particularly for women.

Women are rarely asked this question. And, when we are, we are quick to sense whether or not it is safe to answer honestly. Regardless of how outspoken or even bombastic a woman may be, she may still be hiding what she really thinks until she is in a thinking environment. Don't be fooled by her outward behaviour. For some of us, our survival has depended on keeping the answer to that question to ourselves.

Now we have the opportunity to ask that question all the time and give each other as long as it takes to answer it. In the primal ooze of this question we may be able to create new solutions to old problems and whole new ways to live and lead.

'What do you really think?' is not a question political parties ask their constituencies; it is not one that liberation movements ask their zealots; it is not one the military asks its soldiers; it is not a question companies ask their employees; and it is not a question religions ask their followers. Essentially, it is not a question that shepherds ask their sheep.

In fact, virtually every well-established organization cares more about perpetuating itself than about asking this incisive question. And so we will have to start asking it of each other because our large institutions are not going to do it soon enough.

I once listened to a conversation between two women who were on opposite sides of the abortion issue. They each presented their arguments in detail, one for preserving the life of the foetus no matter what, and the other for preserving a woman's right to choose no matter what. Then one of them asked, 'What do you *really* think about this?'

The other woman did not answer immediately. It was obvious that she was thinking afresh, that something new was about to emerge. The signals are always there in our faces.

'I think we should have no unwanted pregnancies. Then we would not have this problem,' she said.

She went on to say, 'Why can't our society put the same level of resources into finding a way to prevent any more unwanted pregnancies that we put into reaching the moon? Wouldn't it be good if the next president of the US or the EC or Japan announced a goal of reaching zero unwanted pregnancies by the year 2000? I think the money for this should come from every country in the world and especially from churches and religious groups.'

The internal barrier to your power that you have identified, the thing holding you back in your life right now, will be vulnerable to the question, 'What do you really think?' Ask it of yourself now. Don't stop. Ask it everywhere. Be bold enough to answer it.

And when you have answered it, don't expect upheaval. Welcome it.

CHAPTER 10

Appreciation

SELF-RESPECT

Contrary to the messages of sexism, we all have a self. It is a wonderful self, and it is important that we know that. For most women, liking ourselves is one of the most difficult things we ever try to do. Self-doubt, not to say self-loathing, probably lies at the root of all other barriers. It is the one that makes us turn round and march decisively away from our power, as Gloria Steinem argues so well in her book *The Revolution Within*.

We need to find ways to respect ourselves mainly because our greatest tool for change, a thinking environment, requires it. Thinking environments begin with self-respect. They sputter when run by self-doubt, blame, shame, unawareness or chronic apology. For whatever reason, human beings seem to think best in the presence of people who like themselves enough to relax, take their attention off themselves, and listen to the other person unselfconsciously. Similarly, we think better when *our* attention is not tied up in self-questioning or anxiety about what others might be thinking of us.

Not loving the self can so absorb our attention that we do not even hear parts of what the other person is saying. We cannot think broadly while they speak and so cannot offer appropriate support when they reach a point at which they need our help.

Our difficulty in respecting the self can lead us to compete, to try to think of ideas that will make us look good to others or feel good about ourselves, rather than ideas that will work effectively for everyone.

c self-doubt begins very early in our lives. Childhood is gen-
it and miss affair, leaving us strong if we received support, and
of ourselves if we were repeatedly mistreated. We are to be
commended for surviving it. But the damage caused by too much
criticism shows. And we accept the damage as normal; we defend it,
and then pass it on to whoever is next to us in life's queue.

But it doesn't work. We need to face that fact: *excessive criticism does
not work*. It only barricades our best ideas. And it keeps our attention on
how to conform in order not to be criticized, humiliated, or ostracized
further. The very institutions that are most critical of others in the name
of helping them are also the most conformist: schools, medicine, the
military, bastions of government and the Church. A culture of criticism
leads to inappropriate conformity, and conformity of this sort leads to
calamity. Scared of being too different, we go along with practices that
lock us on to a trajectory leading even to the death of our planet.

THE TEN TO ONE RATIO

How much criticism does work? Only a little. A ratio of ten parts
appreciation to one part criticism seems about right. In that proportion
criticism can be very effective. If, that is, the criticism is carefully
thought out and not trivial; if it is the key correction that will positively
affect everything else, it can cause exciting changes in behaviour. But
when the proportion is reversed, when the criticism is ten times that of
appreciation, the human mind halts, defends, escapes or forgets. A
thinking environment is not possible in the midst of too much criticism.

Becoming practised at seeing our strengths, and liking ourselves
enough to stop being obsessed with ourselves and start focusing on new
ideas, takes some specific work. These are many ways to accomplish
this but I particularly like the one I came across by accident when
working with a group of seventeen-year-old women.

YOU *ARE* INTELLIGENT

It was the first workshop in the Young Women as Leaders course. We
had had a good first evening and the group had begun to trust each
other. Being liked had become less important than being real.

I began the class on internalized sexism. My goal was for them to recognize the corrupting effect sexism was having on their thinking and on their lives. I wanted them to be motivated to remove that barrier for themselves.

But all this would require them first to take a deep, critical look at themselves, and at behaviour that had become comfortable and customary, however corrupting it was. I could tell, as they gathered, that there was not a strong enough recognition among them of their strengths and good points to make this possible.

I thought about how to get them acquainted with their strengths. It had to be simple and light, if possible. So I decided I would quickly ask each young woman to identify the quality in herself she was most proud of and then write it in a single word on her name tag. I would then ask her to share the word out loud with the group. I thought the whole exercise would take about ten minutes.

It took three hours.

None of them could do it. They could not think of a single good quality in themselves. It wasn't that they were being particularly modest or fearful of being ridiculed by others who might think they were deluding themselves or being conceited. They really couldn't come up with one good thing to say about themselves.

And these young women were accomplished, popular, influential members of their student community.

But there was no getting round it. They could not see themselves accurately at all. They could see their faults but not their strengths.

So I backtracked. I said, 'There has to be something good about you. You got up this morning and got dressed. That required a certain amount of self-respect. And you were chosen by your school to come on this course. You must have at least one good quality that others recognize in you. Do you agree?'

Blank faces.

'Well, do you agree that you exist, or that at least we are operating on that assumption?'

Agreed.

'And do you agree that at least one other person thinks you are not the worst person who ever lived?'

A few giggles.

'Good. Then, as quickly as possible, non-stop until I call "time", write down every quality you can think of that someone who likes you sees in you. What do they like about you? Make it as trivial or profound as you want to. There are no rights or wrongs in this.'

At the end they all had something on their paper. Their lists included things like kindness, trust, dependability, listening, caring. But every one of them said they did not particularly value these traits. The traits they valued most were the ones they felt they didn't have. Those were qualities like courage, intelligence, beauty, industriousness and articulateness.

Two things struck me: they valued only what they thought they didn't have; and what they thought they didn't have, they had! All those young women were courageous, intelligent, beautiful, industrious and articulate. But none of them thought so.

So I asked, 'What is the quality you most wish you had but you think you don't?'

I asked Ellen to tell me her word.

'Intelligence,' she said. 'I just wish I were really intelligent. I wish I didn't always wonder if what I was saying sounded stupid.'

The other workshop participants vociferously protested that she obviously *was* intelligent.

But Ellen's conviction that she was stupid would take more than compliments to shift. Only *she* could change that destructive attitude. Somehow *she* would have to get into the internal source of her self-doubt and change it. None of us could do that for her.

'Where did you first get the impression that you were stupid?' I asked her. 'Tell me your immediate thought.'

'From my brother,' she said. 'He is a gifted child and I am only normal.'

'Who told you that?' I asked her.

'The teachers and everyone, ever since we first started school.'

So I asked her, 'If you found out that actually you and your brother are equally intelligent, what would change for you?'

Ellen smiled and then laughed and I knew she was considering the possibility.

After a moment she said, 'If I really knew that, *everything* would change for me. That would be amazing.'

We worked together on that incisive question for about fifteen minutes and Ellen agreed to keep open the real possibility that she was at least as intelligent as Jim.

Other participants worked in similar ways and eventually the idea that they all had many admirable qualities, especially the ones they thought they did not have, became more palatable. From that positive perspective we could then look at the changes they wanted to make.

One of the reasons a thinking environment is important is that, within it, even very old, deeply entrenched attitudes can begin to change. When we are given the time and the right kind of attention, and are asked questions that remove the barriers between us and our real qualities, we can begin to see that we already *are* the things we wish we were. And, knowing that, we can start *living* those things instead of longing for them.

YOU *ARE* BEAUTIFUL

More than half the participants in that workshop (and, shockingly, in virtually every other workshop I've run since) chose 'beauty' as the quality they wished they had but thought they didn't. I find this shocking, not just because I wish women would no longer be so preoccupied by this age-old issue, and not just because worrying about our beauty is exactly what male conditioning wants us to do because it keeps us from thinking about things, like power, leadership and organizational change, but because women *are* beautiful already.

Every woman is beautiful. No matter what size she is, no matter what shape her face is, nor the number of freckles or wrinkles or spots or arms or legs she has, she is beautiful. Until women can see this, we are putty in the hands of the very powers we want to change. When we look at each other, we need to see beauty and reflect it back to each other. It is bad enough that every time we walk across the office or into a pub or through the streets the conditioned eyes of men are scanning our bodies for thrills and flaws. We must not do this to each other as well.

Wouldn't it be wonderful if every single time you met a woman, you could be sure that she would regard your looks favourably and be interested in who you really are and what you think and want and feel? The jealousies that make women compete with each other only distract us from our real selves and keep us fruitlessly focused on men.

Where do your standards of beauty come from anyway? They most likely come, not from you, but from magazines, TV, and other people's comments. 'Isn't she gorgeous?' you hear someone say about a particular woman from the time you are very little. You see photographs of models and actresses and hear men and women alike saying definitive things about their looks – 'She's a dish' or 'She looks like the back of a bus.' Every aspect of ourselves, our faces, hair, breasts, bottom, skin, teeth, and fat cells are judged and discussed by other people all the time, based on absolutely no objective criteria.

Who is to say that smooth milky skin is prettier than freckles or wrinkles? Who decided that big blue eyes are prettier than almond-shaped dark eyes or that a 36-inch bust is lovelier than 26 inches or 55? And why is 9 stone the magic weight or blonde hair sexy? There is nothing objectively true about these standards. They are arbitrary. They create deep insecurities in women, and they separate us from each other. Don't believe them any more.

You are beautiful. Right now. Just as you are. You do not have to do anything whatsoever to become beautiful. Your beauty is enhanced only by better health, not by changing the way your body was designed. If you knew this, unwaveringly, what difference would it make to you?

Sometimes women interested in leadership development object to my raising the issue of physical beauty. It is irrelevant, they say. True. It is. And that is why I raise it. It *is* irrelevant. But we don't seem to know that. We spend too much of our time, money and attention trying to look different. The worst thing is the *amount of mental attention* we devote to our looks. I often wonder what we would be thinking about if we were not obsessed with our appearance.

I was consultant to a young professional woman once who said that if she weren't concentrating so much of the time on whether or not her stomach and thighs were too large, she would be developing new product lines, writing articles, talking more widely to her staff and increasing her customer pool. Those seemed to me to be four good professional reasons for stopping her looks obsession.

One of my dearest social-change-political-activist friends (a group for whom beauty is passionately never on the agenda) said she shocked herself when one day she decided to ask herself the question, 'If I absolutely knew I was beautiful, what difference would it make?' She said she had refused to ask herself this for years because she was certain that beauty was not an issue for her. She had always known that she was a plain, unattractive, functional woman. She also said she knew she could never admit to her feminist friends that she ever thought about beauty.

However, asking the question, she realized that she actually thinks about her 'unattractiveness' most of the time. Imagining that she was beautiful (which she is), she saw worlds of time open up for her. She decided, too, that she would no longer steel herself against the silent criticism she had always assumed was there from both men and women and that she would just relax and enjoy people instead. She had spent as much time and thought privately dismissing society's definitions of beauty as other women had spent conforming to them.

Taking the issue of beauty into a thinking session can be very fruitful. Think about it again for yourself. If you absolutely knew that you were beautiful, what difference would it make in your life?

We know now how alarmingly widespread body obsession is and how much of our leadership potential it is strangling. If you haven't yet read Naomi Wolf's book, *The Beauty Myth*, do. It extends the connection between the ceiling on women's leadership and our body fixations by showing that, with every rise in women's power, we are told that we must make our bodies smaller and thinner. We therefore channel our money, time and attention into that task. Obsession with our beauty increases as a way of forcing our real power into decline.

It is now well known that 31 per cent of young American women entering university vomit every day to stay thin. The figures in the UK are similar. I once had a client, Tina, a woman in her twenties, who described parties she and her friends had in their teens. When one set of parents had gone out for the evening, the girls would all gather at that house and each eat 10,000 calories as fast as they could. Then they would throw it up together. They called them 'bingeing parties'. These were high-achieving girls on their way to university and careers. Their parents never found out. Tina stopped when she began to throw up blood.

Our agreement to be obsessed with our appearance and to judge other women and ourselves harshly begins, like most departures from our real selves, early in our lives. I asked Caitlin the incisive beauty question. She could hardly bring herself to think about it. She said that some people say she is pretty. But she hates that because she feels she doesn't have the right to be pleased with her looks. She says she is afraid to let her face show under her long hair or wear anything but an extra-large sweatshirt and jeans. I asked her if she could create the feeling of being pleased with her looks.

Before she could speak, a look of fright and confusion crossed her face and she said, 'I can't do that.'

And then she told me a story she said she thinks about every time she looks in the mirror.

'This guy called Craig was my babysitter. I was ten I think. He came over after school three times a week and about a month after he started coming, he started playing with me in a wrestling sort of way. At first we both laughed and he pretended to be pinned down by me and called me funny names.

'And then one day, almost as part of the play, he lifted my dress and started rubbing my tummy, just lightly, and kept laughing. A few times later he did the same thing, but then he put his hand into my panties, and one day he put his finger into me. I don't remember how I felt. I can't exactly remember what happened next but another time he did that, and then he undressed me completely and rolled me around on his hard penis. That time he told me that if I ever told anyone about this, he would deny it and people would think I had made it up and call me crazy. He did this five or six times before he left for college and we found a new babysitter. He said that the reason he was doing this to me was that I was so pretty.'

She cried. And we talked for a long time.

Eventually she was able to realize that her being pretty was not the reason he had molested her, that she was not in any way to blame, that he had done it because he had, even by the age of 17, been conditioned to believe that his power lay in overpowering others and particularly in 'having' the bodies of girls. She was pretty and that fact was completely separate from his behaviour. Her beauty was hers, not his. Now she had only to enjoy it, let it shine, and know that in itself it could cause no damage.

'What difference would it make in your life if you could be pleased with the way you look?' I asked her a few weeks later. She said she wasn't sure. 'I suppose I'd do more things. I'd meet more people. I might even write.'

Whole projects can be jettisoned because we have been made not to like the way we look. Our thinking stops before it even starts.

YOU *ARE* GOOD

The fact is that you are a person just as legitimately as anyone else in your life. If you believe in respect and encouragement for others, you have got to believe in it for you, too – for you, first. Do you know that moment on an aeroplane, when they say: 'In the unlikely event of a sudden drop in air pressure, an oxygen mask will fall out of the overhead compartment. If you are sitting next to a child or someone else who may need your assistance, *be sure to fit your own mask first*'?

I like that moment because I think that is actually how life works. You can't be any help to anyone in the long run if you try to fit their mask while holding your own breath and growing fainter by the minute. You'll probably get their mask stuck over their eyes and fall dead in their lap in the process.

Appreciating yourself and others is equally difficult. When you have trouble with one, you have trouble with the other. Practising both will help. Before you go to sleep each night, think of someone you love. Make a mental list of the qualities in them you most appreciate. Then the next morning, before you get up, think about *you* in the same way. Make a mental list of the qualities in you that you most appreciate. Then, during the day, tell your friend what you thought about them the night before. Don't let them protest; make them just say 'thank you'. And at some point in the day take yourself out for a cup of tea and tell *you*. Don't protest, just say 'thank you'.

You deserve this. And, if you truly appreciate yourself in this way, you will think more fluidly, more profoundly and more efficiently about every issue you face. Barriers to your power will give way to confidence and energy. In the final analysis, you are the person you must love best in the world. You are the most important person in your life. Others in your life will come and go. But you have you forever.

CHAPTER 11

Feelings

As we challenge the barriers to our power, our feelings will surface. We will need to handle them well, not re-submerge them, but not be dominated by them either. This will not always be easy because we have been carefully taught to be strong, and that being strong specifically means 'rising above' our feelings. One of the things that confounds a thinking environment is the listener's discomfort with feelings. We need to know what to do when feelings arise.

You'd think, to listen to society's displeasure with feelings, that nature had made a mistake. You'd think that crying was not a recovery process and that trembling when we are frightened was not good for us. You would think, especially if you consult women's conditioning, that saying we are angry was harmful. You would even think that talking, just saying how we feel, was not one of the wisest things we can do.

Generally our colleagues and friends would rather anaesthetize us than listen to us express a feeling. When someone starts to cry, most of us try to stop it in any way we can. We offer distractions – 'Why don't we go shopping?' We offer drugs – 'Have a beer'. We offer platitudes – 'You know it will all turn out fine; it always does.' We offer advice – 'Well, what I always do in these situations is . . .' We offer reproach – 'I thought you were braver than this.' We offer abuse – 'You shut up or I'll really give you something to cry about'. And we offer oppression – 'I should have known this would happen if I gave this job to a woman.'

We don't need to do all this. There is nothing to be alarmed about. Nature did not make a mistake. Releasing our feelings is a good thing.

We need to do it every day, in one form or another, and preferably with someone who understands that the process is healthy and finite. It will end – sometimes in a few minutes, sometimes in a few hours. But it is not a slip off the 'deep end'.

We need to let our feelings go for a number of reasons. The most important one in the context of this book is that our minds depend on this kind of regular unclogging in order to work well. Emotional release is part of the complex way that thinking works. And it is part of the ongoing process of removing the obstacles to our power.

I am sure you have noticed that when your feelings are rising but not released, you don't think as clearly or as boldly as you did before. Your ideas become repetitive; they stray from the main point of the discussion; your attention wanders. You cannot think creatively, nor listen dispassionately.

Thinking effectively requires that we allow our bodies to let go of the feelings they have stored up. If you feel sad, cry. Cry until you can think again. And when you feel bad again, cry again. In fact, just tell the person with you what you need. One woman I know said in the middle of a conference call, 'Now I may cry during this, but don't worry; I can cry and talk at the same time.'

If you are angry, say so. Determine what you are actually angry about. Then decide to change your situation to take back your power. Anger is usually a sign that you are being victimized in some way. Facing your anger, you will have ideas that are far more workable than any you could have thought of by denying or 'leaking' or attacking others with your angry feelings.

If you are scared, the same principle applies. Say so. Let your body shake if it needs to, or yawn, or even laugh. Fear is diminished in these ways.

Your brain works better when your feelings are systematically aired. As one young friend of mine put it, 'Go ahead and cry. It will shorten the feeling.'

Gender conditioning makes it hard for both men and women to feel things. Men can't cry because they will seem like women. Women can't rage because they will seem like men. Men can't be afraid because real men just aren't. None of us can feel strongly for fear of seeming crazy. Until we give ourselves permission to rediscover the fact that we have feelings, and that it is fine to let them go, none of us will think well enough.

Our socially conditioned reactions to feelings are strange. We can cry if we just do it for a minute, until our tear ducts fill up but not until they run over. If we are men we can't even cry that much without risking our manhood. If we are women, we can cry a little but for the wrong reasons – proving once again that we are weak and can't be trusted in a crisis. (That one has amused me ever since I first noticed that women handle crises all the time and usually better than men. Men fall apart but people rarely notice because women are there putting them back together again.)

Neither gender is allowed to tremble, even a little. The minute we start to shake, male or female, someone sticks a whisky in our hands or lights a cigarette for us, or rushes us off to a psychiatrist who gives us valium. Men, though, are further abused for trembling – they are called women. Real men aren't afraid, remember. And real men see women as fragile and needing rescuing when we are scared.

Anger is for men. Real men can do it with impunity as long as they don't draw blood or break bones. A furious man, as long as he stays a few feet away, is being manly. Not delightfully manly, but manly. A furious woman, on the other hand, is a bitch.

In her wonderful book, *The Dance of Anger*, psychologist Harriet Goldhor Lerner points out that our language condemns angry women 'as 'shrews', 'witches', 'bitches', 'hags', 'nags', 'man-haters', and 'castrators',' but that 'our language – created and codified by men – does not have one unflattering term to describe men who vent their anger at women. Even such epithets as 'bastard' and 'son of a bitch' do not condemn the man but place the blame on a woman – his mother!'

My colleague Gill pointed out the other day that men professionally disdain women's crying because it makes men apprehensive, but that there is no similar professional disdain towards men's anger even though it makes women feel at least as apprehensive.

Other releases like laughing – Norman Cousins popularized this as a component in cancer healing, and a good one, too – are a bit more permissible in our society. In fact laughter is generally regarded as essential in a good personality and the gift of wit is said to be a sign of intelligence. We like to laugh and to make others laugh – until we overdo it. The really good kind of laughter, the kind that nearly convulses us, the kind that makes us hot and turns to tears and keeps going with the slightest encouragement, that delicious laughter we keep hoping will happen again, is not all right. That is too much, and too much is just too much.

The same is true of yawning. Yawning is very good for us. And, as far as I know, yawning has no gender stigma. Men and women are both allowed to do it. It is not unmanly or unwomanly to yawn. But it is rude. As long as we cover it up and apologize for it, don't do it while anyone is talking, and do it only once in a while, no one disapproves.

And then there is the undramatic act of perspiring. We do this for a number of reasons and one of them is that we are scared. The good thing about perspiring, as far as society is concerned, is that it is silent. The bad thing about it is that it smells. Fear perspiration is especially smelly. And although no one has worked out how to suppress our perspiring reflex the way they have suppressed crying and raging and talking, they have invented powerful anti-perspirants with chemicals that slam our sweat ducts shut and probably do all kinds of long-term damage to them. No one uses anti-perspirant on their forehead and face, though, so sometimes we do suffer the humiliation of people knowing we are afraid.

Talking is fine. About certain things, and to a certain degree. Subjects that are not usually fine are the interesting ones, the ones with the potential to open up feelings: things like death, sex, incest, serious illness (especially cancer and AIDS), class, race and war.

Too much talk is also unwelcome. Even in talkative cultures, there is a threshold beyond which it is rude to go. And in white Protestant English culture the threshold is very low indeed. As with laughter, too much is just too much. It is a sign of something undesirable in a person. Passion, probably. So, it is all right for us to talk, but only about what doesn't matter much anyway.

As a thinking partner, you will want to be relaxed about all these disallowed emotional responses. When they start to happen, resist being alarmed. Just let them happen. They are no different from breathing or coughing or stretching. They are part of our physiology. More important, they are part of our thinking. Without them our thoughts dry up. Thinking is actually a very juicy experience. And feelings are where some of the juice of thinking comes from.

Most of all, don't grasp for something to do. If they cry, don't try to make it better. It already is better. Just stay attentive. Touch the person if they permit it. But don't go into repair-at-all-costs mode. Nothing is breaking. In fact, on the contrary, healing is happening. Crying, as it clears our thinking pathways, probably even makes us more intelligent.

But a thinking environment is not an emotional free-for-all. The release of feelings does not have to be done at anyone's expense. You don't have to yell *at* someone in order to yell. You don't have to cry devasting things *at* someone in order to cry. You don't have to frighten others in order to tremble. You can be thoughtful as you do these things. Your brain does not come to a standstill when you are feeling things strongly. You can still use discretion and kindness as you let go of the venom or grief or terror.

How do you feel about feelings? The best way to find out is to watch yourself the next time someone starts to cry. Notice how you respond. Anything other than relaxed acceptance and encouragement, if appropriate, may mean that you have been treated badly for your own feelings over the years. Can you remember how you were treated as a child for crying or being angry? What did people do to you when you admitted being afraid?

In a popular book on caring management I read a paragraph about the importance of accepting tears at work. The male author was endorsing a 'progressive' attitude that was now policy in an office somewhere. The director of the 'progressive' office was reported as saying that he never fires a woman for crying. Instead, he hands her a box of tissues and leaves her alone in the office to cry until she 'regains control'. This is not a step forward. It reminds me of what a friend once said about token progress: if you take too small a step forward, you fall over.

A thinking environment is a fine balance. Between extremes, taking it all in, the human mind conceives best. We feel as we think. When one begins to outpace the other, we must stop and do whatever is necessary to restore the one left behind. If we are consumed by feelings, we can release them and come back to the balance that lets ideas flow well again. If we are in a cerebral rut we can climb out, notice our feelings, and move to our centre again. To think is to feel is to think is to feel. They are one process. It is when they start to split that we need to take notice.

Keeping an intellectual and emotional balance means that we can usually choose how much we do of one, and how little of the other. When we are listening to someone, their thinking will improve if we choose not to get emotionally involved in the possible outcome of their ideas. We can be keenly interested and have no personal emotional investment in what the outcome will be. This detachment (not disconnection) allows the thinker to continue exploring and not have to stop to take care of our feelings.

When you become emotionally invested in the outcome ￼
thinker's ideas, you lose the ability to hear what she is saying a￼
notice barriers, to ask incisive questions, to appreciate her, to find
key area of improvement for her, to keep her thinking better and
better. The minute you care too much that a particular thing should
result, you corrupt the thinking session and vastly limit the potential for
new ideas and action. In the long run, you will both be happier if you as
the listener do not sabotage the session with your own emotional
agenda.

Your attitude can instead be one of great interest, encouragement,
and engagement in her finding an idea that will benefit everyone. Put
your emotional investment in the emergence of a new, completely workable, wonderful idea.

To be sure you can operate at this level of riveted detachment, you
will probably need a daily emotional outlet for yourself. Be listened to
regularly, as you review what feelings arose for you during the day;
what feelings are hampering your thinking about your life. See if every
day you can cry a bit, identify your anger, or face your fear. Be listened
to for 15 minutes every day as you think and feel. And do the favour in
return. It will make thinking sessions more fruitful and you will be much
more relaxed about others' feelings as they arise. And they will.

Detachment is NOT disconnection...

CHAPTER 12

Encouragement

A thinking environment is by definition a place of encouragement. Encouragement is like a switch. When it is on, thinking flows. When it is off, thinking stops. The effect of encouragement is that direct.

Many of us can trace our achievements back to someone who encouraged us. Often it is just one person who has made all the difference in our overcoming obstacles and ultimately succeeding. We remain eternally grateful to that person for those few wonderful words.

On the surface that seems like a marvellous thing. But I find these stories of the helpful teacher or parent or mentor a bit sad because they illustrate how rare encouragement is in our lives. The fact that one or two people stand out among the thousands of others actually suggests that the majority of people in our lives either discourage us or ignore us. Wouldn't it be better if there were so many people encouraging us we couldn't possibly name them all?

Encouragement is also sometimes regarded as dangerous. I have heard people say that pointing out people's limitations is kinder than encouraging them because encouragement might push them 'beyond their real potential' and cause them to fail.

Nothing could be further from the truth. Encouragement allows people to go forward with fewer obstacles and at their own pace. Real encouragement is never an obstacle.

In a thinking environment every signal has to be a variation on 'Yes, you can think well about this.' Encouragement comes in many forms. In any interaction, ask yourself the question, 'Is what I am doing at the moment offering encouragement to this person?' If it isn't, change it. If you don't know how to change it, ask the person. She will know exactly what you can do to encourage her. You'd know if someone asked you.

This does not mean that you encourage any old behaviour. It means that you encourage people to keep thinking for themselves until they find ideas that will work for everyone's well-being.

One moment of encouragement turned the corner in the establishment of a well-known women's health network a few years ago. Lindy had an idea for a place where women could think for themselves about their health and be treated with respect and with up-to-date medical attention without charge. The motto she proposed for the centre, 'Be the only one who decides what happens to your body', had been a central principle of her teaching in women's circles for years.

She had told two people within an hour one morning that she would need to raise over £400000 to secure the building needed for this project. The first person she told gasped and said, 'Oh, Lindy, do be careful. You may never be able to get that much money and you don't want to get over-committed and then have to pull out. Why don't you find a different place that doesn't cost so much or that you could rent?'

The second person she told said, 'You have everything it will take to raise that money. Why don't you double it and aim for £800000 so that any unrealistic estimates you may have made will not trip you up later? Your project is excellent and will speak for itself. I know someone you should talk to about it.'

Lindy did raise the money. And she says that as she looks back on that period she feels those two minutes of encouragement from that second person made all the difference in her ability to think clearly and boldly enough to convince donors of the value of the project.

Encouragement enfolds people and feeds them long after the event. They draw strength from it far out of proportion to the amount of effort it takes for us to give it. Something this easy we should do more often.

CHAPTER 13

Equality

If I know that you value my thinking as much as I value yours, I can think well with you. If I know that we respect each other mutually as human beings without regard for our status, we can help each other think for ourselves and afresh. You may be the department head and I the cleaner. But if we sit down to think together, as two people mutually committed to thinking anew, eager for each other's success in this, we can achieve it.

Every signal we give as we listen must indicate this equality. In this enterprise we are peers. Our tone of voice, our words, the expression on our faces, the way we sit, and most of all our sustained interest in each other as thinkers, must be those of equals. If you think I am capable of thinking well, then I can think much better. If you disdain my mind or experience or gender or job or background, if you look down on me or if, conversely, you look up to me and feel small beside me, neither of us will be able to think well.

Think for a moment of someone you look up to, even someone who makes you feel small or invisible. If your job were to think with that person about some big issue, what would you face inside yourself? How would your view of them affect your ability to think?

What would have to change in your own mind so that you could think as that person's peer? And what would they need to do in order to reinforce your new view of yourself as their peer?

A common way of destroying a thinking environment through lack of equality is by forming élite groups or cliques. If you belong, you can feel good about who you are. You can continue to keep others out in order to suppress the bad feelings you have about yourself. You sense that if you let in people who are 'less than' you, the 'better' people may somehow see you as one of the 'lesser' people. But if you let in the 'better-than-you' people, you will feel bad about how 'little' you are. And so your energies are directed towards narrowing the 'membership' as much as possible. Virtually no productive thinking can take place in these élitist groups. And, yet, virtually all important decisions about world issues are made by people in just such inward-looking cliques.

Feeling 'less than' or 'more than' is a thinking deterrent. We deserve the joy of living free of both anxieties. Stripping ourselves of them can sometimes be fun and needs to be done every day. As women, we carry conditioned feelings of inferiority when we are with men. In our hearts, we are required to see men, just because they are men, as superior beings. Sometimes this makes us defer to men, and sometimes it makes us copy them. In the one case we play out the worst of our conditioning; in the other we emulate the worst of theirs.

These attitudes will change when we attack them at their roots, and that will mean digging down to the most fundamental, ultimate expression of gender inequality – the concept of deity as male. It is here that we define our most basic nature. The most insidious expression of men's superiority can be found in this ludicrous idea that the god you worship is male. Why this is ludicrous is perfectly obvious (do you really think God has a penis?) and yet even many feminist-identified women defend the use of 'he' and 'him' to address their god. When we do this, we stop short of perceiving ourselves as fully equal to men and we express this acceptance of our inferiority by stopping short of our own empowerment.

To challenge the deeply rooted acceptance that we are not equal to men, I recommend you take a year's sabbatical from calling your god 'he', and call it 'she' instead. In doing this, your most fervently denied assumptions about your own lower rank in reference to men will surface. Many women who have done this have been shocked to discover how deeply they distrust women and how much they depend on the alleged superiority of men. Women who have been progressing perfectly well in their growing independence and strengthening of self-esteem, even the women who have been admitted into the control towers of power, women who fight fiercely for women's inclusion in all policy, planning, and decision-making groups, even women who think men are not to be trusted with life-shaping decisions and who refuse to be intimate with them, can still somehow find their greatest refuge, morning and night, in uttering the words, 'Heavenly Father'.

Every time women do this, we grind into a deeper and deeper level of our unconscious a belief in our inferiority to men. Every time women say, 'Our Father who art in Heaven', or 'Hear, O Israel; the Lord our God is one Lord', we speak lies about ourselves. We say, in effect, that the ultimate power over life and death, the ultimate all-knowing and wise source, the greatest comforter and healer, the one from whom we derive our identity and being, the one and final being to obey, the entity deserving of worship not just love, the one to whom I prostrate myself and the one I hope to serve for all eternity, is male. Each time we do this, and some women do it many times a day, we block the building of a world of mutual respect and mutual power. There is no way we can achieve true equality when we say 'he' to mean 'God'.

Theologically, of course, there is no way a god can have gender and still be infinite and boundless. But the point is that to keep reiterating maleness in our invocations of our god is to collude with our own oppression in the most extreme form. Maleness in our god is, I think, the ultimate denigration of our femaleness.

If you have been calling your god 'he' for some time now, you may protest that you do not think of an actual man when you say 'he'; that when you say 'he', you think 'light' or 'ocean' or 'vroom' or 'blah'. But I doubt that. Images accompany words. If our religions did not want us to associate maleness with our god, they would have used a different word. If they wanted us to think of a genderless, formless, non-corporeal power, instead of choosing words like 'him' and 'lord' and 'king', they would have chosen genderless words like 'one' or 'its' or 'encompassment' or 'omniscience'.

It is hard not to think 'male' when you say 'he'. But more important, saying 'he' almost automatically ensures one thing. When you say 'he', the one thing you do not think is 'she'. And until you can just as easily think 'she', and imagine female as the holder of all power and truth and life, you are admitting to and worsening a deeply indoctrinated sense of women's inferiority to men.

In the long run, this ultimate conviction of the maleness of the Almighty will push you back on to your knees at the feet of men. What you assume to be true, in your innermost heart and mind, will finally dictate your actions.

Try it. Refer to a female god. Even if you are not religious or church-going, speak of your god as 'she' for just one year and see what happens.

In doing this, some women have found that deep down they really believe that men can do the most important things better than women can. Some have discovered, to their surprise, that they prefer to defer to men and not take ultimate responsibility for life and death issues. Some have found that they like being dominated and wish to stay little girls protected by their angry or loving fathers. Some have had to admit that they don't actually trust women, that they worry that women – through inherent weakness and fallibility – will as leaders betray their trust. The male-invented spectre of Eve has slithered right into the deepest crevices of many women's brains.

This change is essential, I believe, if we are really going to stop co-operating with our own disempowerment. Male conditioning tries to keep us powerless. But our conditioning agrees to let it. We may not be able to dismantle male conditioning soon enough, but we can dismantle our own. Could you stand to see yourself as the same gender as your god? Could Jesus have been Martha? Could you stand to see your femaleness as competent, trustworthy, loving, good and wise enough to be God and to come to earth as God's only-begotten daughter?

And, no, I do not think we should worship a female god and start replacing our images of penises and beards with breasts and vaginas. I think that worship, if you choose to worship, should probably be gender-free.

But the real point here is not a religous one. It is a point that is completely fundamental to the issue of organizational leadership – that in letting our gender be the gender of our god, we can finally purge ourselves of our internalized sexist self-denigration, and from this depth of change can see our own worth and power. Perhaps we should also take a one-year sabbatical from imagining our leaders as male. Can you picture the majority of leaders in your company, in your family, in your governments, as female?

From that vantage point we can form thinking partnerships with men, and begin to think afresh, with the certainty and vibrance and competence that come from true equality.

CHAPTER 14

Diversity

'If you were to think about this problem as a proud Malaysian woman, what would you say we should do?'

So began one of the most interesting business meetings I've ever attended. The idea was to see what new ideas might arise if we bypassed the stifling self-doubt created by racism. Valerie went on: 'If you believe racism, you believe that as an Asian or African or Lebanese person you cannot think about important things. That is what racism says. If you believe sexism, you believe that women cannot think brilliantly because that is what sexism says about women. The same applies to any group that has been the object of oppressive attitudes. And of course most of us have many group identities and so are convinced several times over that we can't think. As a poor lesbian Latina Catholic clerk over the age of fifty and in a wheelchair, I probably shouldn't even be able to string two thoughts together coherently. But I can. Occasionally even more than once a week.'

People made a list that day of all the groups they identified with who have been discriminated against. Almost everyone listed more than fifteen. All these groups had been conditioned with virtually the same message about thinking. In one form or another the message was 'You can't think.' And it went on to say, 'The dominant group will have to think for you.' The consequence of our believing this message is that we try to think *in spite of* being black or female or working class, rather than because of it. This means we think from a position of shame, and shame is a powerful thinking inhibitor.

This means that we try to think in the same way as the dominant group in the hope that they will recognize and applaud us for doing so. And that means that we consider only a very narrow range of approaches to any problem and that huge pools of human intelligence become inaccessible. The solutions to the problems stay largely unworkable and dangerous.

Looking at their lists, people next chose the group they most strongly identified with. They then met in like groups, women with women, Korean with Korean, young with young, etc, and considered a problem the organization was addressing. But they did so entirely from the point of view of pride in their group identity. They tried to think about the problem as consistently as possible in the context of the positive cultural aspects of their group – how the best of Pakistani culture would approach the problem, for example. They could then contribute to the larger group, creating the quality of thinking environment that only diversity can.

It was interesting to see the groups try to stay on course and not regress into dominant cultural thinking or doubts about the efficacy of their group as thinkers. The afternoon was short and much more time was needed to explore the newest, most positive solutions that were beginning to appear as the meeting ended. But that simple exercise of defying internalized oppressive attitudes was promising.

Diversity is important in a thinking environment. But it can make its contribution only if thinking is allowed to take place without shame or apology. The same is true of identifying our internal barriers to power – we need to take pride in our own group identities and we also need the fullness and pride of other groups and identities in order truly to see and remove the obstacles in our way. Homogeneity makes us stupid. So does shame.

Consider a problem in your company or home right now. If you were to think about it within the best of your culture, how would you approach it and what ideas would begin to take shape in your mind? If, for example, as a woman staying true to the best in women's culture, you began to think about the economic structure of your organization, what changes would you recommend?

Everyone has some degree of power where they work. Determine how much you have, and consider using it to create an environment in which people can think afresh about the issue of diversity and can then propose new, unoppressive structures and policies for the organization.

And then convene thinking groups to consider difficult problems from all kinds of different cultural perspectives. If you are all aiming to reach a mutually agreeable goal and beneficial solution, useful things are likely to happen because you are thinking fully *as you* and not through a screen of denial of your deepest self. We think better 'in our own language'. And we think better with each other, the more diverse we are as a group. For our minds to be liberated from the killer elements of internalized bigotry, we will have to practise pride in ourselves.

That can mean gathering in groups of diverse people, claiming fully our various identities, telling each other in tones of self-respect what our histories are, and stating the things we are most proud of about our people and groups. What are *your* identities? What has been the history of your groups over the decades and centuries? What are you most proud of about this heritage? Tell each other and listen with interest and respect. In working together this way you can achieve wider-ranging, beneficial change.

And on a personal level, choose someone who is different from you in background, race, class, age, physical ability, sexual preference or nationality to be your thinking partner. Consider your next steps in claiming your power, and work together to remove the barriers. You will both be able to think better because of the differences between you.

We might all do well to remember something an African American friend of mine said once: 'Pay no attention to the fact that I am black, and never forget it.' This state of ambiguity is part of combating the oppression in our world. On the one hand, to have our minds focused on our differences can keep us separate and unreal with each other and can be the basis for discrimination. On the other hand, not to be aware of our different histories and experiences as oppressed groups blends everyone into the dominant group perspective and make us unreal and disconnected from each other. This challenge both to forget and never to forget is easier, however, the more diverse and aware our circle of relationships is. Often the best way of reaching your destination is the destination itself: love is the best road to love; diversity is the best road to diversity.

CHAPTER 15

Boundaries

'When I am listening to someone, I get so caught up in their problems I cannot think straight. I just want to solve them right then and there for them. I want to rock them in my arms and say, "There, there, it will be all right." I go home exhausted from their pain. And then I worry about them all night and the next day. I have enough worries of my own. I don't think I can do this sort of work with people. It is too hard on me.'

This is one kind of boundary problem: other people's problems become yours, you cannot make a distinction between their life and your life; to help them, you feel you have to *be* them.

'When he tells me how hard things are for him, what scares him and how bad he feels about things, and that he feels better after I've listened to him, and then when he listens so well to me, in fact better than any man ever has in my life, you know, not interrupting me very much or telling me what I think or forcing me to take his advice, I start falling in love with him, and I start thinking about sex and candlelight. And then if we hug after the thinking time together, you know, just to say you're a good person and thanks for helping me, I feel like I want to keep holding on and let things go further. Then when I get home, I feel ashamed and scared about meeting him again. I don't think this work is supposed to be like this but I get really mixed up when I am with him.'

This is another kind of boundary problem: disclosing means disrobing. Our society does not have a large enough vocabulary for closeness. If we feel close to someone because we have helped each other and mutually disclosed important thoughts and emotions to each other, and if this closeness seems more intense than friendship, the only words we have to express ourselves are love, affection and excitement. And the only contexts we have for those words are romance and sex. Quickly we can find ourselves assuming that these close feelings mean we are falling in love and heading for bed together. Difficulty begins exactly here, where the boundaries are violated.

'Now she wants to go to the annual company dinner together and just yesterday she suggested we go on holiday together. She asked my daughter if she would babysit for her. And she thinks I should join the woman's club that she belongs to. I don't want to do these things. I value the thinking we do with each other and I like being friends the way we are, so I feel bad about saying no when she keeps suggesting all these new things. I feel obliged to do whatever she suggests because we have become important in each other's growth and she has helped me a lot. I am starting to think I should find someone else to think with.'

And this is another kind of boundary problem: doing one thing together means being willing to do more. You can't say no because you like her and don't want to seem ungrateful for the ways you help each other. If she suggests, you have to agree. Whatever she wants, you have to want.

Good boundaries make good thinking partners. Boundary-less people, on the other hand, invade the space needed for thinking. They will do anything to keep people happy. They don't have a clear sense of themselves as separate from others. They think they have to accommodate what others want in order to be liked by them. Being disliked feels like death. They climb into others' pain and feel terrible when others are feeling terrible. But usually they cannot feel their *own* pain or expect others to care about it. They hate receiving and love giving. They are chronically over identified – with other people.

Until boundaries are established, a thinking partnership is virtually impossible. If you are boundary-less as a thinking partner, you cannot detach yourself sufficiently from the person to think from a wide perspective. You cannot communicate your own well-being sufficiently to relax the thinker so that she can feel free to put her attention on herself. And you cannot see the barriers and think of the incisive questions to remove them because you are bogged down in being her.

If you discover boundary problems in your thinking partner, you may suddenly feel you want to get rid of her; you cannot think for yourself with her because she wants to do it all for you. You sense that she is not trying to help you think; she is trying to get you to like her. She cannot ask incisive questions or listen well because all her attention is on whether or not you approve of what she is doing.

Setting boundaries means making a clear distinction between yourself and the other person. It means making agreements about what you will and won't do together and what the relationship will and won't include. And it means being prepared to risk estrangement in order to think boldly with each other.

It is possible to open your heart to someone and not fall in love with them. It is possible to be freed of former barriers by thinking well together and not be in debt to each other. It is possible to say no to each other and still be enthusiastic about each other and think well together. It is possible to hug and not think of sex.

A friend of mine with years of experience as a high-ranking civil servant, someone who had had to make distinctions and decisions of all kinds for years, once wrote me a note that said:

I have just realized that when I don't agree with someone, I can just say, 'I don't agree with that.' Full stop. No apologies and no trying to help them feel all right about it. That's it. 'I don't agree with that.' This is going to change my life. Love, Ingrid.

In the office, boundaries are extremely important because they not only distinguish between your areas of authority and those of others; they also prevent sexual harassment at all levels.

To practise setting boundaries, think of the person whose approval you are most afraid to lose. In a thinking session ask yourself the question, 'If I trusted that this person would think well of me no matter what, how would I behave with them?'

Another question to consider is, 'If I stopped worrying about others, what would I think about?'

Ask the question and notice your first answer. Say it. Feel it. And ask the question again. Eventually, decide to make that change and talk about the differences in your life that would result from it.

From now on, try to be aware of the times each day when you identify with other people to the exclusion of yourself. Be aware of the ways in which you hold back your own thinking in order not to destroy the peace or happiness between you. Notice how you assume that you know how others will feel, and do things for them without their agreement. If you can, catch yourself and stop it.

Say what you truly think and feel, and see if everyone goes away. They probably won't.

For some women the main obstacle standing between us and our power is this difficulty in setting boundaries. Because we feel we must please everyone all the time, we cannot pursue our own development. We are forever being dragged back into the role we have always played for other people, and we cannot progress on our own path. Sometimes we identify so much with others that we cannot acknowledge that we exist at all. This tendency is of course severely intensified by the messages of sexism which say, in effect, that women do not matter. It may just take a simple confirmation every few minutes to begin to break out of this. Simply saying 'I do exist' could turn out to be a startling exercise.

Many women have also found it useful to say: 'In this moment I will not give a thought to what a man, just because he is a man, thinks of me.' 'Man' is an important part of this commitment because it is men whom we have been indoctrinated to please above all others. But it also works well with whichever person or role exerts the most influence over you. You may substitute 'mother, my child, my boss, the media, the electorate, my lover, my doctor . . .' The person to whom you give away your power is the person to release.

Setting boundaries makes it possible for people to feel the caring from others and for original thinking to develop between them. Boundaries are not barriers. On the contrary, they remove barriers, bringing us intelligently closer.

CHAPTER 16

Physical Environment

A thinking environment is a moment, a relationship, an attitude, an intellectual exchange, a time to release harmful feelings, a statement of support. It is also a physical place. The more accessible a place is for all physical abilities, the more beauty that fills it, the more comfortable it is, the more cultures it represents in its furnishings, the more in tune with the natural world it is, and the more versatile it is for changes in group needs, the better the thinking will be of the people in it.

The psychologist Maslow was right when he said that when our physical needs are not being met, our attention is on those needs and we cannot focus at a more abstract, imaginative level. Creative thinking is not easy when we are in pain, or when our surroundings are screaming denigrating messages at us. Before we convene, we need to make sure that the place works in harmony with our bodies. Then we need to make it beautiful, orderly, light, and rich in the designs and colours of many cultures.

Thinking in a mess doesn't work. As we look around, we need to see reminders that we are good and valued and worth the effort. If we see filth or piles of rubbish, or if no one has given special thought to the environment, the message we read is that we don't matter and that we are not worth the effort.

Take a look at the environments you work in. What are those environments implying about you? What would have to be done to make them reflect your beauty and creativity, to make them well-organized and comfortable for everyone?

Our thinking places need to radiate self-esteem. The more complex and delicate the subject under discussion, the more beautiful should be the physical environment in which we think about it.

Physical safety is also part of a thinking environment. People cannot think well if they are in danger. It is important for women to remember this. Before we can sort out difficulties with angry men, for example, we must be somewhere safe. We also have to remember that our conditioned pull is to make men feel good and to reinterpret their abusive and threatening behaviour as our fault. We mustn't let that conditioning keep us in a dangerous environment. If someone is threatening you, do not go on talking to the person until you have changed those conditions. Require different behaviour, if you can; go where there are other people, if you can't; leave without explanation, if necessary. In any case, do not try to reason with fury. Go where you can think.

Sometimes a person's primary barrier to her power will be the physical conditions in which she lives, thinks, decides and hopes. This factor is sometimes dismissed as superficial. But it can actually have as profound an effect as any other obstacle to our progress towards our real selves. It is a legitimate and recurring issue. Ask yourself periodically, 'What in my environment holds me back? What is the key thing that needs to change in my environment that will change everything else?'

One of the feminist answers to this question has now become part of our language: 'a room of one's own'. A woman I know who is the only woman on the board of a multinational corporation recently discovered how important it was for her to have a room of her own. She also felt that it was important for her to decorate and furnish it according to her taste which included far more Victoriana than either her husband or her feminist work image was comfortable with. But she finally did it. And that one change in her environment had a huge impact on other aspects of her life. Knowing she had a place of refuge, a place of solitude, a place she could maintain to her own standards, sent ripples of reassurance through her otherwise unsettling, conflict-ridden work. Until then, home had in her case been a harder place to lay claim to than the corporate boardroom.

Another woman went on a course which convinced her that the simple factors of light and space have a strong impact on the quality of people's work. So she decided to increase both light and space in her office. She had a small office with only one window. As she looked around she could see nothing that would allow her significantly to increase the light or space in the room. She thought and thought and then asked herself this question: 'What is the one thing in here that, if changed, would allow all the other changes to take place?'

She was pleased and amused to realize that the one thing blocking everything else was the immovability of her telephone answering machine. 'I have to find a way to move that machine,' she thought. That seemed impossible because there was only one accessible electrical socket. But instead of waiting to find a new place for it, she just removed it and then reorganized the room without it. She decided that she would somehow find a new place for it later. That opened up all sorts of possibilities. Now she could move the desk to the other side of the office, put the bookshelves over there and put a lovely large mirror on the wall where the books had been. She could then put a large lamp with a high wattage soft tone bulb by the wall, near the infamous socket. New light paint, a glass table between two lightly upholstered chairs, and an arrangement of delicate flowers all made the room look nearly twice as large and light as before.

The answering machine problem was solved when she saw an advertisement for a voice message service. It simply consisted of electronic pulses in her digital phone system, so there was no machine needed in her office after all!

Just about anything can be solved when you ask the right questions and don't block out the most creative answers.

Think about what you would need to do to make your home, your place of work outside your home, your car, your garden, your town a thinking environment. If you were to transform one of those places into an environment that spoke highly of you and your family, friends or colleagues, that welcomed you and could help you think, where would you start and what would you do first?

We are good. And everywhere we go we deserve to be reminded of that.

CHAPTER 17

Information

The chances are that right now you make assumptions, based on information you have received from somewhere, that are not true. They may be lies; they may be inaccurate approximations; or they may be honest misinterpretations. But you probably hold attitudes that are wrong and hurtful to you and to others because they are based on incorrect information.

Misinformation helps secure all barriers, including sexism itself. In fact, virtually every kind of discrimination is justified' by information that is not true. Take any group that you know is treated badly by society. What do you actually know about this group? What have you been told about the people, their history, their current struggles, the heartbeat of their culture?

To think well for ourselves we need information we can trust. And sometimes thinking begins the minute a missing piece of information is supplied.

One such moment may well have saved my life. It was during the week I was in hospital following my surgery for cancer. I was twenty-six years old and supposed to die in less than three months. A few days before, I had asked my doctors uncomfortable questions about the toxic effects of radiation and chemotherapy, but they had answered with, 'There are no options here. If you do not do as we say, you will die.' On this particular day I was resting in my hospital bed. No one else was around at that moment. My eyes were closed but I heard the door open and felt someone slip in. I could not see him as he leaned down to speak to me.

'Nancy, this is your Uncle Henry from Oklahoma. As you know I am a gynaecological surgeon. I have come here to tell you something. I have looked at the slides of your tumours. They are very bad. But I have had many patients over these forty years with ovarian cancer this bad. What I want you to know is that as many women get well who just go home as who take chemotherapy.' Before I could respond, he was gone.

I remember thinking at that moment that if all else failed I could always, as he had said, 'just go home'. I also realized that he had come 2000 miles just to tell me that. A new, relaxed confidence set in, and I slept. From that point on, I was able to think for myself about a full, non-toxic health regime that would find me 20 years later alive and robust. With encouragement and correct information that I use to this day, Uncle Henry had effectively created for me a life-saving thinking environment.

People are easier to dominate if they are kept ignorant. And the best way to keep people ignorant is to humiliate them for asking for information. At school, pupils get used to hearing things like, 'If you had been listening, you wouldn't have to ask that. I've already answered that three times today. Pay attention.' In some families children repeatedly hear: 'Don't get clever with me, asking questions all the time. You'll do what I say.' And in some organizations asking for information can cast doubt on your loyalty and can even, on occasion, mean dismissal. In the case of people like Karen Silkwood, it can lead to death.

Make a list right now of all the things you want to know that you have been discouraged from finding out. If you knew that asking these questions until you received satisfactory answers was a sign of intelligence and desirability in a person, what would you ask next?

How have you been treated when you asked questions? Tell a story from these chapters in your life. How should people have treated you so that you would be confident about finding out what you don't know? Who did encourage you to ask when you didn't know?

Whether in business, in research, at school, in childhood, in global planning, in the intimacy of friendship or sex, or in the ordinary challenges of daily life, a thinking environment praises the question-asker, relishes the question, and is patient and generous with the answers. The drive to know lies at the heart of interactive thinking. At the heart of human nature seems to be an undissuadable curiosity. In our trenchant tracks to think exquisitely for ourselves, and in partnership with others, we must encourage each other to do one thing repeatedly: find out, find out, find out.

PART 3

Going Into Action

A political client of mine told a women's conference that one of the most consistently helpful things she does when meeting ministers of state, usually all men, or when being interviewed by the press is to ask herself, 'If I were not afraid at this moment, what would I say?' She is one of the best female self-promoters I know but she still struggles each time with the sexist fear that she is not worth listening to and that the world will ignore her. Going into action with our ideas is harder than it looks. If it weren't, women would be doing it by the millions.

A good idea is no good unless we put it into action. And that takes a level of confidence and sense of self-worth that women, trapped inside our conditioned desire to defer and to promote others, find terrifying. In thinking partnerships we can admit that we are scared, and we can remove this barrier with incisive questions. Then we can take every step necessary to promote ourselves and to stay in the public eye with our best thinking.

In this section I have addressed some of the issues women face as we decide to lead and I have suggested ways in which a thinking environment and an ongoing thinking partnership can keep us focused on our intelligence and power. I like to imagine what we will do when nothing holds us back.

CHAPTER 18

Deciding to Lead

SEEING YOURSELF AS A LEADER

The first time I led a group of people I had to radically shift my perception of myself. I had stood up in front of classrooms before – I had been a schoolteacher since leaving university – so speaking to people with some authority was not entirely new for me. But the first time I was introduced as a workshop leader, I had to see myself very differently.

I remember feeling fine in the period leading up to the event. I had not flinched when the publicity was sent to the sixty people who would be attending. And even on the day, setting up the conference room, I was not nervous.

And then the first people arrived. I watched them through the window of my upstairs room. They unloaded their car, loaded themselves up with what looked like enough luggage for two weeks, and walked into the hotel lobby. I assumed that they had gone straight to reception and registered for the Nancy Kline workshop. It was then that I began to panic.

Why had they come? What did they want from me? Did I have a single reason to think I could deliver whatever it was? They didn't know me personally. How did they know the weekend would be worth their time and money? How could I have been so outrageous as to have invited even one person and charged them even one penny to learn even one smaller-than-you-can-imagine idea from me?

I was a nobody from a small town two thousand miles away and I seriously began to wonder how I had ended up here. Then more people arrived. Within half an hour, forty or so people had unloaded their cars and presumably registered for this weekend with me.

I decided I had to do something. After deciding not to kill myself, I thought I would try to greet the people as casually and confidently as I usually greeted people at a dinner party. That idea appealed long enough to get me down the stairs. I could then tell that people were happy to see me. Some looked more scared than I felt. That was perversely reassuring. Even people I didn't know smiled when I intro- duced myself, so I assumed that they were not disappointed yet.

I walked past the meeting room, and saw the sixty chairs, and many participants beginning to sit and read the material in their folders. They were facing the front of the room where the leader would stand.

The leader. That was when it hit me. The leader was me.

I remember standing in the hall and at that moment, as if suddenly there were no turning back, I knew that I had only one viable choice. Sixty people were here for a workshop presented by Nancy Kline. They assumed I could lead. So I had to assume that, too.

I knew I could do one of two things. I could either stand in front of them and let them see every sniffling doubt about myself, apologize for being born, and squirm under their far-too-generous expectations of me. Or I could stand and say what I had come to say, look them in the eyes, tell them what the workshop would consist of, ask for questions and tell them my answers, and keep my voice loud and tender. I could lift my chest slightly and pull my shaky chin out of my neck. I could move my body as if there were some differences between me and a corpse. I could at least act as if I had something of value to offer. I could point their minds in a specific direction and be firm about what I expected of them. I could even say what I hoped for for the world – I could try to inspire them.

Then I could listen to them and use my skills to get them to see their own power. In other words, I could act like a leader. I could just change my view of myself. I could lead and not apologize.

Then I could wait and see what happened. If they all went home before breakfast, I could decide to move to another part of the country and go into palaeontology. If they didn't, I could . . . well, that would be amazing. If they didn't go home before breakfast, well, I'd just have to think about that. It might mean something too good to think about.

I did walk into that room and down that aisle and stood in front of those people and said, as if I had done it for years and years, 'Good evening, everyone. Welcome.' And I just kept going, deciding over and over again to act like a leader and see if they all went home. They stayed.

Most of us can probably lead better than we think. Our view of ourselves is so far from the mark, it is as if we were two people. We are the person sexism has tried to 'keep at home' and we are the person who, brave and seeing, ventured away from home a long time ago. For women to lead in great numbers, we will have to stop 'returning home' and run instead to catch up with that amazing girl who has already caught the eyes of the world.

Every so often I go into our village to shop and I see Mary with six or seven children all clinging to her, only three of them hers. She and they are often shouting and laughing and standing with their toes over the kerb, trying to cross the road. No matter what the weather is like, she is cheery and the children jump and laugh around her. I always wonder what she would think if she could see herself as I see her – a young, mature figure, in charge, and an inspiration to the people she guides. She is already a leader. But I suspect she would laugh if I told her that.

The very first thing you must realize is that you have already 'left home'. See the impact you are actually making. See yourself as a leader. Assume that people want to hear from you, can be inspired by you, and that you can get things done, while bringing out the leader in them.

WHAT DO YOU REALLY WANT?

This question of questions appears everywhere, and never in a more important place than this. When most people decide to move into a leadership role, they do so with their efforts in one place and their hearts in another. Don't do this. From the beginning, lead the things you really want to lead.

What do you want to lead? Begin by thinking about what you want to accomplish – what do you want to see happen in the world before you die? What issue do you care passionately about? How would you like to see that issue moved forward where you live?

Don't be influenced by fashion. If you feel passionate about damage to the ozone layer, for example, step forward and do something about that issue. But if you don't, leave it to someone else. Decide what you really care about, and what you most want to be a spokesperson for, and do that. There are plenty of people to do whatever needs to be done – that is the one good thing about our explosive population. So, choose from your heart, not from pressure.

And defy duty. You are not obliged to put your efforts into something just because it is a pressing issue. Most issues are pressing. You will make the best contribution if you do what you can do imaginatively, energetically, with conviction and delight. Duty has nothing to do with it. All the world's problems began long before you were even conceived, so you are forgiven for all those things you didn't even do. Choose freely what you lead. The world will see much more progress that way.

If you could trust that all the vital issues in the world are being addressed effectively by large numbers of people, what would you *choose* to lead? What would be fun? If you aren't having fun doing it, if you can't laugh your way through it and dance at least some of the time, you've made the wrong choice and you should get out and make way for people who can.

As with anything important in your life, it may take a little while to answer these questions honestly and fully. Take the time. When you are excited about your decision, you will know that you are on the right track and your work will develop quickly.

MAKE A PLAN

Then you can make a plan. But this is tricky because plans, rigidly followed, rarely work. And that is a good thing. To be in charge but not to control is one of the delicate balances leaders have to strike. This distinction is most important when we are working with other people. We need to be clear and firm but we also need to let go, to cast the meeting or the project to the gathering winds of multiple minds at work together. As leaders we must collaborate, labouring together while keeping our particular contribution well defined.

If we try to control everything, we put out the light that is guiding the group, we kill the seeds of serendipity, and we limit the outcome to only those things our particular experience can conceive of. We cannot conceive of the best ideas on our own. We need collaboration with other people, not control over them. But we also need to stay in charge which means keeping the group or project on course and full of life.

This distinction between being in charge and controlling also applies to our plans. It is good to have an outline of where we think we want to go, with general directions and sometimes a proposed timetable, but a blueprint is dangerous. With a blueprint, you can build a house but not a human outcome. There are far too many variables in human interaction for us ever to be certain of what to do next. And the minute you are certain, you can be sure that you have overlooked many important details or closed the door on the most exciting options. The minute you are sure, you can be sure that thinking has stopped.

So, make a plan, and then 'put it in a drawer'. Be guided partly by your plan but also by the 'inner voice' that will tell you whether you have stayed true to your dream. Open the 'drawer' and check your plan only now and then. The best part will be seeing how wrong you were, how very much better everything has turned out than you could possibly have imagined – largely because you stayed powerful and let go.

THE AMY PRINCIPLE

There will be difficulties. You might as well face this fact so that you can handle them when they arise. These difficulties will be in just about every area. The most draining ones, because they can be the most disappointing, will be those that arise between you and the people you work with.

At the beginning of any group effort we usually hope that everyone involved will be good to each other and will grow together from the experience. But the chances are that the people you start out with will not be with you in three years. And that is not a sign of failure. It is often a sign of increasing maturity and of change in people's directions. Sometimes participating in a project can clarify for people what they really want, at which point leaving becomes a positive step for them.

But sometimes people-upheaval results from a particular mistake we make as leaders. This is the all too common one of wishful thinking. We hope for more from someone than anything they have demonstrated to us actually warrants. We do this sometimes with friends or with people we are particularly attracted to, people who would be fine to spend a weekend with but not to chair a project with. And sometimes we fall into the trap of wishful thinking because a person reminds us of someone from our past – someone we perhaps regret having hurt or some-one who dominated us and to whom we were never able to say 'no', someone in our family who never believed in us. There can be many almost unconscious reasons at the root of wishful thinking and the bad personnel appointments it leads to.

But we can sometimes avoid this trap if we apply what I have come to call the 'Amy Principle'. I was treated to this principle in a context that had nothing to do with hiring or firing people. When I was running a school, Amy, my assistant, and I used to go for a walk together every day during our lunch break. We decided one spring that during our walk we would take turns listening to each other on the subject of our personal struggles against sexism. We would each answer the questions, 'How have you stood up to sexism today?' and 'How have you fallen victim to sexism today?' We would end our turn with, 'What will you do from now on to avoid being a victim that way again?'

We had a wonderful spring examining our lives every day so positively. And we tried to stay true to the thinking environment principles of appreciating each other and listening without judgement.

One day Amy asked me a truly wonderful incisive question. I was talking about a new relationship I was embarking on. I was expressing some concerns about whether or not I could stay fully true to myself and still let myself become completely close to this person. She asked, without fanfare, 'When you think about any difficulties that might arise, what do you *know now* that you are going to *find out in a year*?'

That question, if you can stand to acknowledge your very first answer to it, is ruthlessly well-aimed. It will tell you all you need to know, and more than you can usually stomach, about what lies ahead. She was right to ask it in just that way because we already do know, from almost the first twenty minutes we are with someone, what our key difficulties will be with them. Whether in love or in work, we overlook the obvious because it is more pleasurable to expect the best at the beginning. Sometimes we wishfully think our way through the whole first year. And then the fantasy falls apart and we have to throw out the rubble from the damage that, if anticipated, might never have happened.

As you gather people around you, ask yourself this question as soon as possible. Be willing to listen to the first answer, and take it into account as you proceed. Then ask it again each time your relationship with that person changes or each time you take on a new person. Don't worry – it won't take the joy and hope away from the first few months. But it might well prevent serious disappointment later.

And go for walks with your colleagues. You never know what might come from them.

AVOIDING SEDUCTION

For a woman it is not so much a matter of whether someone will try to seduce her each day but of when and how many times. All forms of seduction are dangerous. Seduction distracts us from our real selves and places us in someone else's frame of reference. Sexual seduction is an obvious factor in any discussion of women and leadership. But there are also other kinds of seduction which are even more dangerous because they are less obvious.

One of the functions of oppressive conditioning is to distract the subordinate group from its power. If you defy your oppression, you will disturb the keepers of the dominant culture, and they will react against you. Fortunately, though, before they try to kill you, they will try to distract you by seducing you. They will try to run you off your road and then spin you round until you can't quite remember where you were going. Then you will find yourself back on their route, marching in time to their drum.

A few years ago my brother, by then an experienced airforce pilot, demonstrated for me the importance of thinking clearly in the face of seductive forces. He used the analogy of pilots trusting their instruments in fog, because in low visibility you can't fly 'by instinct'. He put me in a large swivel chair, one I could fold my legs into and lean back in. He asked me to close my eyes. He said he would spin the chair round and that I was to tell him when he had reversed the direction of the spin, and then to tell him again when he had reversed it back to the original direction.

I closed my eyes and began spinning, and soon I sensed that the chair had slowed down and was gradually beginning to reverse direction. When I was certain that I was now spinning right when I had been spinning left, I said so.

'OK,' he said. 'Now say when you think I've changed it back.'

The same thing happened. I sensed the chair's loss of velocity and then I could sense its change of direction. I said so. Bill said, 'OK, now open your eyes.'

'Was I right?' I asked.

'No,' he said, 'I never did change the direction of the spin.'

I could not believe it. I was sure he was lying just to make me feel stupid. But then I tried it on his daughter and the same thing happened. I never changed direction and she thought I had done so three times.

I have never forgotten that demonstration. It has been a metaphor for me for many things and in particular for the importance of following our 'instruments', our clear perceptive signals, when we are in a 'fog'. This is particularly helpful when we are emerging in leadership and are bumping into male conditioning everywhere. Male conditioning tells us to close our eyes. And before long we are sure that we are on course when we are off, and off course when we are on. Then, when we realize what has happened, we are furious with men for having tricked us. And yet, we are the ones who agreed to close our eyes in the first place.

Part of the function of sexist conditioning is to spin us out of control. We finally make it into the pilot's seat and before we know it male conditioning lures us into a cloud in which we submit to the familiar feeling of pleasing men, of letting them take over again. We forget to trust our instruments, our own minds and experience, and we lose our way. It is a good metaphor because, if we don't open our eyes and look at the control panel in front of us, we eventually run out of fuel and crash.

Watch out for this as you venture further and further beyond the comfortable confines of your previous limits. It does not matter where you have decided to try your wings – home is just as much of a challenge as Parliament, sometimes bigger actually; but wherever it is, be alert to the seductive forces that will come from every direction to turn you aside from your chosen course.

The obvious ones will be the easiest to fight. When male conditioning shouts at you and demands that you stop developing, says you are ruining everything that is good in life, accuses you of taking power and jobs and influence away from men, calls you unfeminine or man-hating or unnatural or a bitch, when men say they will leave you or tell you that you are asserting your way out of a promotion or when they dance you into the night and caress you into bed, these seductive forces are pretty obvious. It is hard to miss them and it is therefore easier to short circuit them.

But the most difficult one, and the one that has distracted thousands of women from fuller and fuller expression of their power, is the one that begins with alliance, co-operation and promotion, and slowly insinuates itself into the very substance of your plans. Watch out for the sexist 'feminist' man, the man who claims to be in favour of your rise but knows better than you how you should achieve it. Watch out for the bit of male conditioning that will applaud you for a while and then explain nicely that you have gone far enough and that everyone will be happy if you can just stop there. Watch out for the man who claims to be interested in women's advancement but does all the talking and rarely asks women what they think.

And watch out for the man who is interested in men's liberation, the man who talks about how sexism hurts him, too (which it does), but equates his liberation with a return to the warrior, the mythical hunter, a spear in one hand and a drum in the other. Watch out for him because his manifesto does not contain a single paragraph on women's empowerment. On the contrary, it blames bold women for what has been wrong in men's lives in these past fifteen years. Male conditioning makes men forget to put women's empowerment at the heart of their search for liberation. And until they *want* women to lead them back, not to the sword but to their laser keen humanity, men will continue to thrash about on their internal battlegrounds of disconnection. Men cannot be free until they turn to women, not to look after them but to lead them, knowing that this will result in a true sharing of power.

And as for sexual seduction, remember that male conditioning counts on female conditioning to want sexual approval more than anything else. Offices, law firms, companies, laboratories and committees worldwide are teeming with women's conditioned desires to be anointed by the sexual sceptres of the men around them. Wherever men and women gather there will always be at least one man who thinks he is the Greek god in the bunch and that the woman he directs his gaze at will be instantly distracted by his greatest of all endorsements – his desire for her.

One problem with seductive sex is that it lets the fog in. Women, inside our conditioning, rarely think well after we have had a fix of external male blessing. And in the fog, we may spin unknowingly away from our hard-won route of power and personal joy. Sex is bliss when it is an expression of a well-developed, intelligent, emotional relationship between real peers. When thrown into the path of professional development, however, it is seduction, and almost inevitably sets us back. Amy's principle comes in handy here. When you first see the haze on the horizon, ask yourself, 'What do I know now that I am going to find out in a year?'

MAKING MISTAKES

It is important to make mistakes. I will be forever grateful to another Quaker friend of mine who once told me that if you aren't making mistakes, you aren't doing anything worth remembering.

Make mistakes. Get out there and try the things you are not yet practised at. Moving out of our conditioned roles and self-images as women will mean making all kinds of interesting mistakes. You cannot know in advance the result of every decision you will ever make. You just have to try it and see. Making mistakes allows something interesting to happen. Nothing new or useful ever emerged from certainty or perfection.

When people begin to express themselves and be heard, they often become more cautious and more perfectionist than ever. This is understandable because the further we stray from the norm, the more heavily criticized we are, and being criticized is not fun. For women perfectionism is understandable because, in order to achieve recognition by a dominant culture, we usually have to do twice the work, twice as well, for half the reward. On this unfairly judged journey, making mistakes can seem too dangerous and costly.

But, in fact, the bolder we feel, and the more soundly we are rooted in our selves, the more willing we will be to be wrong.

Lewis Thomas, the biologist, wrote a wonderful essay on mistakes in his book called *The Medusa and the Snail.* Read the whole essay when you can, the whole book for that matter. It is superb. But remember the following excerpt in particular:

We are at our finest, dancing with our minds, when there are more choices than two. Sometimes there are ten, even twenty different ways to go, all but one bound to be wrong, and the richness of selection in such situations can lift us onto totally new ground. This process is called exploration and is based on human fallibility. If we had only a single centre in our brains, capable of responding only when a correct decision was to be made, instead of the jumble of different, credulous, easily conned clusters of neurones that provide for being flung off into blind alleys, up trees, down dead ends, out into blue sky, along wrong turnings, around bends, we could only stay the way we are today, stuck fast.

The next time you make a mistake, celebrate. And try to find the interesting advance that may come out of it. There will have been at least one.

WOMEN LEADING WOMEN

'Do we have to hurt each other so much of the time?' a female politician asked me one day with hope draining from her eyes.

'I am not going to lead if it means losing you as my friend,' a teenage woman said to her friend at a young women's leadership workshop.

'I got out there and almost overnight all the women closest to me abandoned me. I have never felt so alone in my life. I knew the men would leave. But the women? Why the women, too?'

The heartbreak in these three women should be branded on our minds as we decide to take a lead, wherever and however we do it. First, we must understand why we abandon each other. We do it because our conditioning simply says that women are not as good as men and that men should lead. Eventually, we believe it. When we believe it about ourselves, we then believe it about people like ourselves – about other women.

We believe it when it says that as soon as a woman puts a foot over the line we have drawn for ourselves, she has overstepped those delicate bounds that keep a woman truly a woman. We believe it when we don't think women, in the end, can do a very good job. We believe it when it says that, if *she* can do it, perhaps *we* could do it and that would mean rethinking the comfortable limits we have settled for all these years.

Sometimes it is because we long for the pleasure of achievement and recognition she is receiving but we don't believe we can do things as well as she can; and so decide to diminish her rather than promote ourselves.

But, whatever the reason we have blocked or hurt each other, what really matters is that we do not let it happen again. This does not mean that we have to like each other. It does not mean we always have to agree. It does mean that we have to make sure we think together, that we listen fully and formulate our mutual goals and then keep asking the questions that will take us towards those goals. We must not again sit after the meeting drinking coffee and grinding the woman leader into a powder in order to scatter her to the winds.

We can take our time, slow down and listen to each other all the way through until we can come to real understanding. We must not let the conditioning that tries to destroy us from the inside be the force that makes us hurt each other on the outside. That is not leadership. Real leadership is making sure we keep each other thinking afresh and for ourselves, and that we champion ideas that will work for us all.

There is plenty of leading to do and plenty of leadership opportunity to go around. We do not have to function according to a scarcity model. We'll each have our chance; we do not have to undermine or destroy each other. We do not have to do the work of sexism.

Women can lead each other beautifully. As you take the lead, be sure that the women around you have opportunities to talk about what they think; and find out what they would most like to do as leaders, too. Gracefully allow time for women to appreciate each other openly and individually. And be sure that you hear every day what other women value about you and your leadership.

Leadership does not mean giving up your female friends. Male conditioning has once again put that idea into our heads because men have led in such chilling isolation. We do not have to do likewise.

Take time to remember how lucky we are to be women, how much there is to value in each other, and how much men stand to gain from our refusal to hurt each other. They will be watching out of the corners of their eyes. They long to see a different way.

LIVING YOUR VALUES

A few years ago a woman from an American company phoned to tell me about a conference she had been to for executive women. She was ecstatic. The conference had cost $6000 for each participant and had lasted three days. It was not the lovely venue that had thrilled her, nor the large number of highly accomplished businesswomen there. It was the theme of the conference. For three days they had done nothing but examine one question, 'How can you make your work express your values?' (I questioned the values implicit in charging each person $2000 per day to explore her values, but still . . .)

This question was exciting to her because it is an attack on most of corporate life. Personal values just do not come into the strategic plans of most corporations.

Male conditioning invented the corporation. And everything about it reflects the disconnected, defeat-to-win, control-as-you-lead, don't-be-too-different requirements of male conditioning. The bottom line is profit. The top lime is more profit. Personal values aren't even pencilled in.

But women are scaling the corporate peaks these days. And, before we forget why we are climbing, we need to move our focus away from the ropes and cords, and, through our binoculars, survey the summit. Is that where we want to go? What will we have when we get there? Will the air be too thin to breathe?

As you think about what and how to lead, don't start with the demands of the corporate or public world. Start with what you care most about. And make every decision about your leadership consistent with those values. Women's conditioning has not turned us away from our values. On the contrary, they are our chief consultants and we can let them direct our actions. At each step, ask your values what they think of your plans. And listen.

FLOURISHING

No more superwoman. Please.

You can't add and add and add and add and add and add to your activities and not, sooner or later, die from the strain. Women have always done too much. This is not a phenomenon of the 'feminist era'. We've always worked until we could not work another second and a bit more. Washing machines didn't change that. We just generated more laundry. It is well know that single-parent families are now feminizing poverty. It is also true that the by now stereotypical picture of the wife cleaning and cooking and caring for children after she returns from an eight-hour day at work, while the husband reads the paper and watches television, is no joke. It is prevalent and it is still as dangerous for women's health and women's advancement as it ever was. 'Fine,' these men have said to us. 'You can do whatever you want to to develop yourself, but don't think it's going to change anything I do.'

Frightened, wading through our conditioned need to keep men happy, having no financial alternative, we agree to do it all. And we are doing far, far too much. We assume that the price we have to pay for stepping free of our conditioning is to take care of everything so that no one will be ruffled.

Look at the diaries of professional women, every single minute organized and arranged to take care of every permutation of family and community need, day after day. Many women even schedule sex. 'Five o'clock on Wednesday,' one friend told me, 'but' she said, 'I was so exhausted, I fell asleep. He was furious.' No kidding.

Start again by thinking about you. Do not assume that what you have been doing is necessarily what you will continue to do. Begin with your health. What will it take for your body to flourish? How much sleep do you need in order to feel good? How much time do you need to spend alone in order to know who you are and what you think?

And what would you be eating if you weren't trying to please and prepare for other people all the time? When and under what conditions would you be sexual? How much physical affection would you want if it were right for you? How would you exercise in order to feel good and know you were healthy? Who would massage you and how often? When would you listen to music? What would you be reading? What would you be making? How often would you cry?

My mother used to get an hour and a half to herself in the early mornings before everyone else got up. But, in order to justify it, she had to couch it in good-for-us terms. 'I am not fit to be with until I've had my coffee and read the paper. You wouldn't want to come into the kitchen too early and face me, I promise you,' she would say.

She even made sure that guests and new in-laws understood this rule. It was her sacred time, but she couldn't say so. I just wish she had felt able to say, 'I need time alone and early morning is best for me. Don't come in for breakfast until after 7.30.' But I also realize that her orchestrating time alone in any guise was, for her, a revolutionary act of self-caring. The only person she allowed to break that early morning rule was her little grand-daughter. Laura was always welcome. I think Laura knew how to be herself and that meant that Mother could be, too.

Start with you, before you make too many other plans. After you die, it will be too late.

DON'T JUST PREACH IT

Your daughters are watching. They are learning from everything you do, though they will forget most of what you say.

You could talk without hesitation about what you hope their lives will be like. In general you probably hope that your daughters will have a better life than you have had. You hope they will not be so deeply exploited, nor so easily victimized, nor so frequently disappointed. You hope they will rise further and walk more proudly than you have. You hope most of all that they will be happy.

They probably will improve on your life – children usually do. But your daughters will do so only in tiny steps if you don't start aligning your life as closely as possible with those hopes and dreams right now. They learn what we live. The Quakers were wise again when they said, 'Let your lives speak.'

As difficulties arise and you forget where you are going and why you are doing what you are doing, just decide again to live now the life you dream of for your daughters. That may well be the most effective way of all to challenge and remove the barriers to your own power.

CHAPTER 19

The Thinking Partnership

We are very, very lucky to be women. When I think about our lives and our history, I am always moved and proud. Women have done extraordinary things. We have done them with love and great intelligence.

Our lives are filled with accomplishment. They are filled with the courage to be heard, to be seen, to be taken seriously. In the face of daily oppression we have for centuries and in every society organized ourselves to say to the world, 'We, for our own accomplishments, not just as appendages to men, are important.'

Our lives are also filled with longing, with fragments of goals not yet reached, with dreams that things can be better in our world. We are fully capable of reaching our goals and realizing our dreams. But we live and work in a world of isolation structured by male conditioning which sometimes makes it difficult for us even to remember what our dreams are. We need to establish in our daily lives a particular kind of support that will see us through to the dreams we have and will help us replace our longing with achievement and satisfaction.

In all my years of work with women I have not come across a more powerful force for this level of change than the *thinking partnership*. Seeing it in practice, time after time, I am beginning to think that if women everywhere could establish it in our daily lives, nothing could stop us.

A *thinking partnership* is a relationship with another woman in which you take equal turns listening and thinking. It is a guaranteed thinking environment that you and a friend give each other.

In a thinking partnership you think out loud for fifteen minutes about an issue of importance to you. Your friend listens. Then she thinks out loud about an issue of importance to her, and you listen. It is simple. It is disciplined. And it is near magic.

We think we already do this. But we don't. We think we listen to our friends and colleagues, but we don't; we interrupt them. We think we wait patiently for them to work out what they really want to say, but we don't; we finish their sentences for them. We think we help them think for themselves, but we don't; we give them advice or tell them *our* story.

We think we ask incisive questions like, 'If you weren't afraid, what would you do?' But instead, we ask insulting questions like, 'Does a little thing like that really scare you?'

We think we express appreciation to each other but we don't; we criticize ten times more than we appreciate. We are too embarrassed to say from our hearts what we admire and love about each other.

We think we are thinking afresh, but we are mostly repeating what others have thought. We think we are being honest, but we are often covering up the real issues.

We talk a lot. We have lively conversations over lunch and tea and coffee, at meetings, at parties, at work, on the phone, in the car, in the supermarket; but we don't very often think afresh in all this talk. We rarely listen long enough, and we hardly ever ask incisive questions. We need a more disciplined structure if we are going to think beyond our barriers and habits. This is what a thinking partnership can be.

A thinking partnership can provide a place for you to think things through every day until new ideas emerge. It is a unique time to sit down, to slow down, to breathe for a minute, to be given attention with respect, to go on without interruption, to consider ideas without argument, to take a break from criticism. It is a time when the person listening to you, your thinking partner, shows real interest in *your* ideas, a time when you can see the confidence she has in you, and when you can say and think anything.

You deserve this – a place and time every day to consider your *own* mind, to listen to your *own* heart, a time to work out at long last what *you* really want.

In this partnership you are forced to hear how good and intelligent you are, and not feel ashamed of needing that. In this partnership you brag just a little about how well you have done. You don't feel compelled to give all the credit to ten other people first.

In this time and partnership you have permission to say what is hard in your life, to talk about the pressure you carry inside virtually all the time, to acknowledge the pit of grief in your stomach, to say you are afraid. Your partner will not think you are weak for saying so, nor will she feel burdened or obliged to fix things for you. She will just listen to you and listen and listen some more. She will ask you an incisive question here and there to remove the barriers in your thinking, and then she will listen again.

And your partner will never gossip about what you have said, so you can venture even into subjects you have not dared consider.

A thinking partnership can be added to a friendship and will enhance it greatly. But it can also be built with someone who is not necessarily a close friend.

A thinking partnership is important because everything you do comes from the thinking you do about it beforehand. Action is only as good as the thinking behind it, and when we don't take time to think, we take action instead day after day that harms ourselves and our world. Conversely, when we do take time to think clearly, we make better decisions with greater benefit to others.

WHAT WOULD YOU THINK ABOUT?

What would you think about right now if you had fifteen uninterrupted minutes? What if you had a friend who would sit with you, look at you, smile at you, pay respectful attention to you, and not interrupt you while you talked? Imagine that she would listen so well that you could, without rushing, come to new insights about some problem, that you could feel much better for having talked about this issue, and that you could begin to do something effective about it. That would be fifteen minutes well-spent. And what if you could return the favour and also listen that well to her?

What *is* on your mind today that you have not had time to think about well? Many issues press down on us. In our women's population, for example, 92 per cent of us could be leading more publicly than we are now. Maybe you would want to talk about what you would be leading if you were not holding back.

Most of us have lived our lives doing what others want us to do. Maybe in a thinking partnership you would want to ask yourself over and over again that unsettling question, 'What do *I* really want?'

A huge number of us are over-extended in our lives, repeatedly promising far more than we can deliver, exhausting ourselves and going to bed at night feeling guilty for not having done enough. Maybe in a thinking partnership you could practise saying, 'No.'

As many as 8 per cent of us know the joy of being lesbian but the agony of living in a world that condemns that choice.

Statistically, 37 per cent of us are in continuous conflict in our marriages, a surprising number of us still having no decision-making power over the money in our families. If this is true of you, maybe in a thinking partnership you could think about how to change that.

A shocking 82 per cent of us spent part of our childhood in emotionally damaging, sexually abusive or addictive families and are chronically frightened to say what we *really* think. Perhaps in a thinking partnership you would just want to speak about *anything,* to practise not censoring.

A huge number of us have been pregnant against our wishes. An unknown percentage of us have had abortions with the added pain of being under legal threat for this action. Too many of us are agreeing to unnecessary hysterectomies and mastectomies. Young women are the fastest-growing population with the HIV/AIDS virus. Perhaps in a thinking partnership you could consider being from now on the *only* one who decides what happens to your body.

Many of us are watching our daughters struggle to define themselves in our still male-dominated society. Many of us are watching our sons unwittingly play out that domination in roles they are told to repeat just because they are men.

Most of us are challenged to make ends meet in economic systems which seem perversely unsuited to human thriving.

Maybe in a thinking partnership you would want to talk about these things and to think about what you would do about them if you were not afraid.

All of us are, or have been, angry (at least once!) with the person we love most. You need to know that you can talk about that, too, move to the other side of the fury, and think well as a result. You need to know that you will not be misunderstood for facing that anger and for thinking for yourself afterwards. Maybe in a thinking partnership you could do this.

In every nation women are facing a time of profound change and upheaval. Old values are under new scrutiny. Controversial policies, which will have a particular impact on women's lives, are in the making. Much better policies will emerge if you can think about them first in thinking partnerships and always in a thinking environment.

Thinking partnerships are a place for considering every issue facing our world. Thinking partnerships provide the conditions under which we can think well so that we, as individuals and as nations, can stop making the same mistakes and begin to do things better.

But thinking partnerships are also for celebrating.

For example, you are a leader. You have inspired, you have designed policy, you have helped expand the economy, and you have raised the next generation. In a thinking partnership you should recognize successes like these. What have you done just recently that was successful? Whom have you told? And what have you accomplished over your lifetime so far that you are most proud of? Take the credit. The successes in our lives are staggering.

As women we have been made to feel apologetic for ourselves, made to feel that we haven't done anything particularly noteworthy, and that whatever we have accomplished is probably not as impressive as the things men have done. This is a lie. In a thinking partnership we can remember what we have done well. We can then be reinforced in our strengths and can think even better as a result. The higher our self-esteem, the better we can think.

Any subject, large or small, is fair game for a thinking session. You can start wherever you need to, to examine your life, your leadership, your organization or your country, to think of new ideas that will work, to plan next steps, and to appreciate yourself. In a thinking partnership you have the chance to let your own mind work as well as possible. And because you are not alone, you are less likely to suffer the stupidities that breed in isolation.

As one woman put it recently, a thinking partnership is a place to be yourself.

WHO IS THE CENTRE OF YOUR LIFE?

This all seems simple enough. But if it is so simple, why do we have such a hard time doing it?

The answer is clear. We have been conditioned as women to believe that we are here to serve others. We forget that *we* are 'others', too, and that we must serve ourselves as well. We put our thinking time last because we put ourselves last.

Every day most of us live in a vortex of activity, most of it based on the unexamined idea that others are more important than we are. Even in this era of women's advancement, women are still taught that we are here to serve others *at the expense of ourselves.* It is not unusual for us to look up now and then and find ourselves spinning out of control on the periphery of our lives. We agree that we will take time for ourselves only when everything is all right with everyone else. We plough through our day assuming that what *we* want is selfish; we assume that what *we* dream of is idealistic; and we work till we drop just to keep things running smoothly for other people.

One of my colleagues said it well: 'I live my whole life as one big attempt to get people tucked in at night. I feel that once they are taken care of, I can get on with the other things I want to accomplish. But by the time everyone is tucked in, I am so exhausted, I can't remember what it was I thought I wanted to do.'

In this compulsion to help others we are also in an enormous hurry. We drive too fast, we attend too many meetings, we talk too fast, we jump to hurried conclusions, and we jump into each other's sentences, finishing them for each other as if this were the last minute on earth to make our point. We live as if every moment were a crisis. And people cannot think well in crisis.

Thinking partnerships stop you in your tracks and force you to put yourself first for a moment. They are a statement that you matter. In fact, a thinking partnership is a revolutionary act for women because our oppression tells us that women cannot think, that men will think for us even about *our lives,* and that time spent thinking for ourselves and about ourselves is time wasted. This of course is another lie. Women can think brilliantly, and there is no group whose thinking time is of more value to the world than ours.

But it is no wonder, given these messages of sexism, that women are at first hesitant to set up thinking partnerships and commit to thinking time in their day.

To combat these messages we have to plan our thinking time first, *before* we schedule anything else: before meetings, before extra work hours, before children's doctor's appointments, before church services, parties, care for our ageing parents, the washing – before *every-*

thing. We will have to schedule our thinking time *first* in order not to find ourselves coming in last.

DO IT

We need to meet every day with another woman and take time to think for ourselves. Fifteen minutes a day should be our goal. Thirty minutes would be even better. But even five minutes can sometimes work a miracle. The key is to be the centre of attention for your full turn, to think for yourself and not follow anyone else's agenda. Begin this right now.

Think of a woman you know. Think of someone you like and trust. She may be a close friend, a colleague, a sister. Let it be a woman who won't gossip about you. If possible, choose someone who is different from you and who is your peer. Phone her today.

In your own words, and with your usual style of banter and fun together, tell her about a thinking environment. Be explicit but not formal. Include the points that give the thinking time its disciplined quality, emphasizing that a thinking session is different from a chat. But present it so that it will sound as appealing as it actually is in practice.

In your words, tell her that you want to try listening to each other for at least fifteen minutes a day once a week for about six months. Say that it will be simple, fun and confidential. Tell her that there are six agreements you will need to make with each other:

1 Equal time:
   You will each have equal time to think about your life, your goals, the barriers in your way, and your next steps.
2 Only *incisive* questions:
   You will ask each other questions, not out of prurient curiosity, but in order to remove barriers in your thinking.
3 No advice:
   You will give advice *only* when it is asked for directly at least twice.
4 Permission to feel:
   You will encourage each other to cry, laugh or tremble when you need to.
5 Wholehearted appreciation:
   You will appreciate each other specifically and sincerely.
6 Absolute confidentiality:
   You will not tell a soul what you hear.

When you meet for your first session, explain to her in more detail what a thinking environment is. Be sure to emphasize that when she is listening to you, she must keep her eyes *always* on your eyes and maintain an interested, unworried facial expression. Tell her also that she must not jump in and finish your sentences for you or comment on what you are saying.

Give her examples of incisive questions and show her how they are different from other kinds of questions. Explain what a thinking barrier is and how to remove it with these questions.

Get her to practise with you and don't be afraid to correct her. Tell her you are doing this so that you can have an uncorrupted partnership from the beginning. Relax about this because she will be glad to learn the most effective way to think with you. Keep the ratio of appreciation to criticism at ten to one, but don't allow something that is wrong to go unchecked. A thinking environment is exciting when it is right and pointless when it is wrong.

Think of your first month's thinking sessions as times of teaching and learning. Let them also be times when you adapt the process to your particular cultures, countries and social groups. Don't collude with the oppressive elements in your own culture, but do improve on the process as I have described it by making it consistent with the best in your cultures.

As a white, middle-class, United States middle-aged, able-bodied woman, I will have designed this process with many limitations as well as strengths. Even more humanity, flexibility, clarity of thought, and ease are emerging in the thinking environment processes of black women, young women, lesbians, working-class women, women from the southern hemisphere, women in wheelchairs, women in their eighties. We need to listen, ask incisively and encourage. But the precise way we do that varies enormously from culture to culture.

Just keep your objective clear: equal time to think for yourselves and afresh about your goals and about the barriers in your way. Be sure that you both leave the session encouraged and reconnected to your power and intelligence. Reaffirm each time in a concrete way how good it is to be women.

Some people have found it helpful to follow this simple series of steps:

1   Find a quiet, private, pleasant place to meet
2   Notice something positive about each other and say it

3 Set a timer or notice your watch and make sure you each get the same amount of time
4 When it is your time to think:
- first talk about your success and the good things in your life
- then explore your goals and the key barrier in your way
- allow yourself to cry or laugh or tremble if feelings surface
- plan your next steps in meeting your greatest challenge
- appreciate your partner
5 When it is your time to listen:
- appreciate your partner
- keep your attention on her all the time
- listen for her goals, notice her barriers, and *when she has finished talking,* ask questions that will take away the barriers
- express interest and delight with your face and eyes and words
- relax when she cries or laughs or trembles
- remember her goals until you meet again

Tell your friend from the beginning that you are not expected to join in each other's activities or projects but merely to listen, ask and encourage. Remind her that the partnership agreement is just for six months so that each of you can teach and enjoy a variety of partners. This, of course, can change if you both want to continue the partnership. I have been thinking partners with the same three women for five years now.

Remember your appointments with each other, and be on time. And, again, insist on competence from each other – if your partner judges, comments, advises or criticizes you, show her how not to do it. If she fails to appreciate you concretely, ask her to. If she turns up on your doorstep every day expecting the world from you, tell her to go home. Respecting boundaries and agreements keeps the thinking in a thinking environment.

Most of all, enjoy yourselves. Be more and more adventurous in these sessions. Think about the things you've put off thinking about, the ones you've been too scared to think about, or that you always thought someone else could think about better than you could.

And remember to let each other cry. Don't pat each other to death in the process. Just be there with each other, touch each other if you agree to that, offer a tissue, and remind each other that the taboo against emotional release is rubbish. Help each other to keep going, even to cry harder, until you can think afresh again.

Once you have made this process work with one woman, consider inviting another friend to be a thinking partner with you, too. This way it is possible to have a thinking partnership almost every day. And the differences in your partners will enrich your experience.

Will men do? Women often ask this question. Yes, of course, thinking partnerships are good with men, too, but not as a replacement for a thinking partnership with another woman. Women need a place where we are not pulled to please men or to say what will make men feel good. Women need a place where we can consistently put ourselves first, as women, and work out what we *really* think and want. Only then can we know what we would do on the other side of our barriers. With women we can find ourselves and not get sidetracked so readily in the search.

GLOBAL IMPLICATIONS

There are clearly many personal reasons for establishing a thinking partnership in your life. But there is also a global reason for forming thinking partnerships and thinking environments wherever we are. Women are at a crucial stage in our development and in the history of the world. At this juncture, we can provide a model of a new kind of leadership. We do not have to lead as men have led. They have had to lead this world from inside the prison of male conditioning. Inside this conditioning they have been models of leadership in which what is right is what is strongest, what is best is what defeats and what is real is what you cannot feel. We hate that conditioning, and beneath it, so do they.

Eventually women *will* be 52 per cent of the leadership of the world. We *will* set policy. We *will* create economic and political structures that work for the good of all people. We are moving in that direction steadily. But we will do so well enough only if we can think *afresh* along the way.

Women can change for the better the way people lead. The President of the Republic of Ireland, Mary Robinson, spoke of this opportunity in the opening address she gave to the Global Forum of Women. She said:

Through their community sense, women may well be establishing a new kind of leadership: one that does away with the traditional relationship between the individual and the group, one that is enabling and empowering of the individual and the group. When women lead, when they contribute and articulate their purposes in a society, it seems to me increasingly that the individual woman and the community of women work together in a fresh and radical way. This method of dialogue and co-operation blurs the old distinctions and heals the old divisions.

As women, we still have time to build our leadership from our humanity and to steer away from male conditioning. We still have time to think together so that we come up with new ideas that bring our world back to its heart.

It will take courage, and we will need each other in order to stay on track. We will most of all need many thinking partnerships in our lives.

This daily support for yourself becomes more essential the more visible you become as a leader. Each time you decide to make a change that even slightly challenges the male-conditioned *status quo*, you will probably be assaulted by people who find your actions threatening. These assaults are really nothing to worry about. But they can be discouraging because they can make you question what you are doing, and they can knock you back into old, self-demeaning ways of interpreting your world. Eventually they can, if you let them, cause you to give up.

The very best protection against these hapless flailings from the hard-dying habits of sexism is another woman who listens to you, helps remove your barriers and encourages you every day. This is real support.

Real support is committed to our finest thinking, to our success in reaching our own goals. Real support is sharp, loving and dependable. It is far more than a gripe session and far more than sympathy or collusion with helplessness. We know this as women. But we need now to be organized and intentional about it. And we need to take on the issues of our power and leadership and extend our support for each other beyond the haphazard events of daily life. We need to do this even more dependably as we become more prominent. We must let our supportive women's culture become a conscious, systematic method for the development of improved leadership in the world.

CHAPTER 20

Women's Thinking Groups

The one thing as good as a thinking partnership between women is a women's thinking group. Essentially this is a collection of thinking partnerships meeting to encourage each other in large numbers.

If we are going to restore human thinking to the highest possible level and if, in particular, we are going to change leadership so that it is capable of taking the institutions of our world back to their humanity, we have to give ourselves permission to be inspired by what women have done and are doing day in and day out.

We are leading; we must hear about it. We are learning vastly important things; we must teach each other. We are savouring and preserving life; we must celebrate. We know what is possible, and we must remind each other.

The annual women's conference, the task force, the monthly speaker, the women's executive retreat is not enough. We must inspire one another at a much deeper level. The women's thinking group can do this. The thinking group must include every woman, not just the celebrities and the talkers. It must meet often and be structured as a thinking environment to give each woman a chance to review her challenges, take pride in her achievements, and make plans for her next steps. It must also be a time of remembering and sharing the ways in which we have fought sexism in our lives.

Most of us in the Western world do heroic things isolated from other women's achievements. We may be in the physical presence of women but we do not communicate specifically about our achievements and plans *as women*. We may work on commercial projects together or gather in children's playgroups together or attend academic classes together. We may even serve on women's political or religious committees together. But we don't take substantial time together to reflect positively on our lives as women and to gather collective strength in our struggle against sexist conditioning.

Eventually this isolation makes us forget that millions of women are doing the same sorts of amazing things all over the world all the time. This isolation makes us question our perceptions and lose our nerve. Women's thinking groups are one very effective way to come back together to inspire and remind each other.

Like the thinking partnership, the thinking group is simple to set up. The group can be any size. Sometimes it will consist of many thinking partners coming together, say, once a month. The initial requirement is simply that they know about a thinking environment or be willing to learn. Thinking groups seem to need a minimum of two and a half hours, the time to be divided into three sections:

1 Ask everyone to talk about something positive in her life and to share one way in which she recently stood up against sexism. Make sure that everyone has a turn and that everyone listens with the same high calibre of attention that she is accustomed to in the thinking partnership.
2 Give everyone at least thirty minutes to talk about her key challenge as a woman and her next steps in meeting it.
3 Let each person be appreciated by everyone else.
   Set the time and meeting place for the next group.

When the group is larger than five, split up into smaller groups of three or four for Part 2. This is much better than shortening each person's time to less than half an hour.

This is a very rough outline of what a women's thinking group can be. Even if it is never any more than this simple structure, profound things can happen for each woman. You will inspire each other and you will look forward to the next time because you know you will receive excellent attention yourself and that you will make a difference to each of the other women. You will be surprised at how much your stories and challenges will mean to the others.

You could also try talking occasionally about your personal histories as females, and about women in history and in your field of work who have inspired you. You can also talk about the challenges in your personal life and see how they relate to the public ones. Usually, when we compromise our power at home, we also compromise it in public life.

When people first hear about women's thinking groups, some are reminded of the consciousness-raising groups of the sixties. Thinking groups are different – although they also raise a good deal of consciousness. A thinking group is essentially a larger version of a thinking partnership, focusing on successes and next steps, not just raising our awareness of sexism in our lives. It is a way of empowering women, not just a retelling of our oppression.

It is vital to structure the group so that everyone gets a turn and so that the questions require the women to view themselves positively and to realize how far-reaching their decisions and actions have been. Guest speakers are fine, but they can't do this job for us. We must talk to and hear from each other in detail, and give specific and well-aimed appreciation.

I would like to see thinking groups convened all over the world to explore how every major social system in our lives can be more fully human, and freer of male conditioning. We especially need thinking groups to tackle and change economic policy so that we can find systems that will work. The old ones are self-destructive and not nearly good enough. We need to go beyond corporate capitalism, beyond collective socialism, beyond charismatic leadership and far beyond the oppressive systems of military juntas, outdated colonialism and crazed nationalism. No system currently in place on a wide scale is good enough for human beings. In women's thinking groups we can begin to understand and to rethink all these systems.

Men can eventually join us – after we have learned how not to let male conditioning take over, distort, or limit the possibilities. I remember a group of five women leaders meeting informally many evenings in a row at a long conference. We gathered on sofas in the coffee room after the day's work was done and talked about it all. Most of the time we also made sure that we asked each person what she thought needed to be different the next day so that the conference would be more successful.

One evening, one of the men leading the conference asked if he could join us. He was fascinated by what we were doing. I think it had something to do with the sofas, our floppy, tired bodies, the laughter, the sharpness of our ideas, the ice-cream, and the conspicuous absence of a flip chart. He was quiet and afterwards said he had had a wonderful time, that in fact he had never experienced anything like it before. I thought this was unwarranted enthusiasm for such an ordinary event. I see now, though, that he suddenly found himself in a completely different culture, one without male conditioning.

He asked if he could come the next night, and the next. He was clearly enthusiastic about meeting this way. By the third evening he had begun to say more and to add to our ideas. But by the fourth he said more than anyone else, by the fifth he took notes and by the sixth he started the meeting himself. By the last day of the conference he essentially ran the meeting. Our original structure had disappeared completely and we were lifeless after the day's work. A few months later the women reconvened and talked about it. It wasn't hard to work out what had happened. Sexism in all of us had taken over. But at the time our internalized women's conditioning had found it too hard to stop him.

So, as women, we need to value our thinking sufficiently and stop revering male conditioning sufficiently to keep women's culture strong in our meetings. Then we can invite men to join us. Men who want this, and who look to women to set the thinking standards, will be excellent thinking partners with us.

CHAPTER 21

At Work

Over the years I have repeatedly been asked to write a step-by-step guide to creating a thinking environment at work. I have resisted because I believe that only *you* can know the very best way to introduce these principles into your own life. I am also aghast at the idea of people following a textbook of 'thinking rules'. Lover of oxymorons that I am, I don't find this one amusing; indeed, I think it could be very dangerous. But an outline of suggestions need not be seen as a book of rules or even an instruction manual.

So in this chapter I offer some ideas for setting up your workplace, your home and your relationships as thinking environments. I am keen to hear how you apply them, what works, and what you do that improves them. Going on thinking environment workshops and courses may make it easier to learn how to apply these principles in your own life. But even without them, you can improve the quality of the thinking around you and the quality of your own thinking and living.

I see people applying these ideas at two levels. At a formal level, the ideas can be discussed, learned and used as official procedure and management style. At a less formal level, you as an individual can change the culture of your workplace and home by behaving in accordance with these principles yourself.

CREATING A
THINKING ENVIRONMENT FORMALLY

DETERMINE YOUR
SPHERE OF INFLUENCE
. . . .

At work you may be formally designated as, for example, manager, group head, director or consultant. But even if you are not, you do command a sphere of influence, a circle of people who depend on you or look to you for direction, or help, or who will at least listen to you and consider what you say. Work out who they are. Make a list of their names (and, if possible, the names of the people whom they influence). The people you directly influence will be the ones from whom you select your first thinking group. Set yourself the goal of turning your sphere of influence into a thinking environment within a year.

SELECT A SMALL GROUP
. . . .

Choose no more than six people who are most likely to be interested in the principles and process of creating a thinking environment. Some people are particularly inclined towards this level of human interaction. Some may have been allowed through their childhood to retain a natural interest in other people, and some may have been specifically trained in the art of communication. Some will also take an interest because their professional field is human development. Some will be interested because they respect and trust you. Regardless of their reasons, if they have an interest in improving human interaction your initial work with them will be easier. The tougher attitudes can be tackled later.

DISCUSS THIS BOOK TOGETHER
. . . .

Tell them you are interested in setting up a thinking environment and are inviting them to join you in the first stages. Then set up several discussion meetings over a period of weeks to review the ten principles described in Part 2 of this book.

● Use the principles even in these discussion groups: hearing in the beginning from everyone about the good news in their lives; giving everyone a chance to speak throughout the discussion; hearing people's own examples; inviting questions and original thinking from them; and appreciating each other.

● These discussions can take as little as half an hour and will still achieve a lot. They may have to be over lunch or tea, or even before work over breakfast or coffee. They do not necessarily have to involve a huge new investment of time. Often people find that after the first meeting they are eager for more anyway and will gladly set aside the time. Some say they are more efficient and energetic during the day after the meetings and that no real work time has been lost.

● During this period of discussions, agree that you will practise between meetings what you have read and discussed and will report to each other next time on your progress.

● Keep the appreciation ratio at ten to one.

INVITE ONE PERSON
FROM YOUR WORKPLACE
TO BE YOUR THINKING PARTNER
. . . .

This person does not necessarily have to be a member of the discussion group. You can set up a weekly time together and agree to try it for six months. The previous chapter on thinking partnerships will be a good guide for you in this. This person should be someone you respect and enjoy spending time with. Remember that talking on the telephone can sometimes be as effective as meeting in person, and can often make your thinking sessions possible despite problems with schedules or transport.

SELECT OTHER MANAGERS
OR GROUP LEADERS TO BE
FORMALLY TRAINED IN THE PROCESS
. . . .

You may want to do this in the same way as you introduced it to your first small group. But it may now be possible for you to have them formally trained as part of their paid staff development.

In order truly to incorporate the principles of the thinking environment at work, you need to redesign the current forums for professional interaction.

STAFF MEETINGS

Begin the meeting by giving each person a few minutes to say what is going well in their life or their work. Insist on a wholly positive report. We think better about the negative factors in our work if we first put our minds on what is going well. Make sure that each person is given respectful attention and that what people say is not judged, laughed at, or discussed. You should also ensure confidentiality.

When leading a meeting, present the issues clearly and make concrete proposals that the group can then reject or approve. Avoid asking vague questions like 'Well, how shall we start?'

At the beginning, give everyone a turn to speak before the general discussion. Periodically stop the discussion to hear from everyone again. Some of the best ideas come from the quietest people.

If the group is larger than eight, split up into smaller groups at least once to give everyone some time to comment and think out loud. No one should leave a meeting having been silent the whole time.

Take particular notice if those who are not speaking are from minority groups or otherwise traditionally silenced groups. Make sure you draw them out.

Summarize clearly what has been decided before the meeting ends.

Also before the meeting closes, ask each person to comment on what they feel has been achieved and to appreciate another person there.

INTERVIEWS

In order to get the best thinking from your job applicants, you need to reduce their fear.

To this end you can:

Give them beforehand the key questions you will be asking them.
Greet them with a smiling face and make eye contact.

Set the room up in as relaxed a way as professional boundaries will allow.

Have everyone on the interviewing committee as well as the applicant say something good about their worklives at the beginning of the interview.

● Break any tension with benign humour.

● Appreciate them genuinely at intervals during the interview.

● Periodically check your facial expression to make sure that you are not scowling or looking worried or critical without realizing it.

● Ask unannounced incisive questions that will begin to remove barriers, such as: 'What is the key thing holding you back from the level of work you would like to be doing? If it were magically gone, what would you do first?'

APPRAISALS AND
SUPERVISION MEETINGS
. . . .

● Begin with a long list of what you think is going well in the person's work.

Then ask the person to say what they think is going well.

Ask them to say in what ways they think they have improved.

Ask them to identify the key thing that they think needs to change. The key thing is the change that will positively affect almost every other difficulty. When people are asked to focus only on the key thing, they usually think less defensively about the changes needed and come up with self-motivated ideas for improvement. There is nearly always a key thing that will affect most other things.

Then tell them yourself what you think the key change is, and suggest ways for them to make the change.

Keep your voice relaxed and your attitude hopeful even while you say things that may be difficult for them to hear.

● If they cry, relax, listen, and continue when they can think again. Do not interpret crying as weakness.

● If, on the other hand, they stiffen and withdraw, back off, listen, relax and let them 'return' at their own pace.

● Take time now and then to ask them what they really want in their work life and listen to them think about how to achieve that. Keep your own views and preferences out of this discussion.

Make sure you have listened to anything else they may have in mind.
● Appreciate them before they leave your office.

PROBLEM-SOLVING MEETINGS

Help people find their *own* solutions. To this end, you can:

Ask them questions and listen.

Note the barriers in their thinking and remove them with incisive questions.

Be sparing with advice.

Suggest they focus on the *key* problem – the one that could solve the rest of the problems.

Discourage compromise; instead inspire people to find a new solution that is good for *everyone*.

POLICY-MAKING MEETINGS

Convene a policy-making group of representatives from the organization.

First say what is good about the existing policy.

Next determine the key thing that needs to change.

Make your own concrete proposal for change.

Then ask for a proposal from each person, without allowing any response or criticism from other members of the group at this stage.

Discuss the proposals, hearing from each person at least once.

Determine which proposal the group favours.

If the group has policy-making power, make a decision. If they only have consultative power, appreciate everyone for their ideas and relay them accurately to the policy-making group.

LONG-TERM DEVELOPMENT MEETINGS

Convene groups (of twelve people or fewer) to think about the organization's long-term development. Make the groups as diverse as possible; and draw on people at all levels of the organization, including the part-time and lowest-paid workers.

Open the meeting by hearing from everyone about something good in their lives.

Begin the discussion with positive assessments of the organization's achievements to date and its vision for the future.

Ask people to say what they would do to express the organization's vision if they were in charge.

Ask them to consider what the organization might do differently if it expressed its vision in ways consistent with each person's culture.

STAFF LEADERSHIP
DEVELOPMENT MEETINGS

Look at each person on your staff as a potential leader.

Set up a meeting with each one to listen to them talk about their dreams and goals. Keep them thinking beyond their doubts or conditioning. 'What do you really want?' will be a crucial question here. Do not make suggestions unless asked.

Reshape your departments and divisions as people's leadership develops.

Encourage people to be trained and developed according to their next leadership steps.

● See to it that all leaders in your sphere of influence, including you, are appreciated every day by the people they are leading.

● Set up a leaders thinking group for yourself with other leaders in your field who are not in your direct area of responsibility. These people might be outside your company but will have something in common with you. Examples I've come across include the Executive Women's Group, Managers in Publishing, Head Nurses, Heads of Voluntary Organizations, Directors of Small Schools, Mothers Under Thirty, and Pharmaceutical Company Division Managers. Gather in whatever grouping reflects your common experience. Meet in small groups (of not more than six) in order to share insights about your work; to talk – even cry – about what is very hard in your life; and, most important, to think specifically about your goals and next steps, and to appreciate each other.

STAFF SUPPORT GROUP MEETINGS

● Institute weekly staff support group meetings, lasting at least one and a half hours, paid for by the organization if possible.

● Encourage everyone to run the group along thinking environment lines but allow for great diversity in the type of support people can request. I have even known staff support groups to be focused around swimming together, driving, grieving, reading in silence, sharing feelings about a TV soap opera, listening to music, walking, drawing and writing.

● Let the priority be the giving and receiving of equal time and attention.

FOUR KEY WAYS TO IMPROVE MEETINGS

1 TAKE TURNS TO SPEAK

In all meeting situations, the most important thing you can do – even if you do nothing else – is to take turns. This one change can make lasting differences in the way people think together, in the quality of their interactions, and in the restoring of their power.

2 ASK INCISIVE QUESTIONS

The next most important thing is to ask the kind of questions that remove barriers in people's thinking.

3 APPRECIATE EACH OTHER

And the next most important thing is to appreciate each other often and specifically.

4 CREATE A COMFORTABLE PHYSICAL ENVIRONMENT

Use whatever influence you have to make your meeting room beautiful, clean, light, spacious (even with limited space), reflective of the cultures represented there, inclusive of nature in as many ways as possible, and personal. Make it genuinely smoke-free and quiet. Encourage people to use it at other times to find a calmer pace, to remember their goodness and value, and to rest.

The other components of a thinking environment also matter a great deal. But these four are its blood and guts. Or, more accurately, its heart and soul.

CREATING A THINKING
ENVIRONMENT LESS FORMALLY

Whether or not you can readily change your staff or organization into a thinking environment, you can informally influence the people around you by living according to these principles yourself. Specifically, you can begin to:

Practise the ten to one ratio of appreciation to criticism wherever you are.

Slow down and pay attention to people.

Listen without interrupting or rushing people.

Ask questions that remove the barriers in people's thinking.

Smile.

Make your posture, facial expression and tone of voice as welcoming and interested as you can.

Resolve not to joke at someone else's expense.

Stop being alarmed when people cry; listen to their feelings warmly and dispassionately.

Sing.

● Change your physical environment so that it becomes clean, light, comfortable for everyone, and includes natural objects and things of beauty.

Know the groups represented in the people around you; find out all you can about their histories, achievements, their conditioning, their heroines and heroes, and their holidays.

Giggle.

And don't forget, your family is an organization, too, and will live more successfully and happily if it is largely a thinking environment. The chances are that you are the chief executive there. You have a wonderful opportunity to make it a thinking environment. The same principles apply to families as to any other organization.

Your personal relationships are also potential thinking environments. These principles work beautifully on a one-to-one basis, even at the deepest level of intimacy. Relationships that are generally thinking environments are not only intelligent; they are also sensuous and scintillating. In the end, the quality of your closest relationships will determine the quality of your leadership.

Periodically ask yourself, 'Is what I am doing right now helping this person to think?' If it isn't, go back to the principles, and change what you are doing. You will probably notice a difference immediately.

CHAPTER 22

Go Where the Dancing Is

Feminist writer Nicci Gerrard has commented that in this next period of women's empowerment 'accusatory shouts', 'war manuals' and 'ambushes' won't be our only effective strategies. Women's equality must permeate the whole fabric of society. In our efforts to draw the world differently we must put the facts, the analyses, and even our anger in a wider context.

We are trying to build a better world, not just a different one. And to do this we need strategies that embrace 'peace, pleasure, doubt and joy' as well as fierceness, strategies that – while keeping women close to each other – also include men. In this next thrust of change, we must remain firm and determined, but we must also, as Nicci Gerrard suggested, go 'where the dancing is'.

This approach is one that includes everyone, where we think afresh together at the same time as marching side by side, where we take the time each day to recognize and remove the internal barriers so that we can permanently topple the external ones. In this 'dance', joy is not poisoned by fury; we will think not as sophisticated victims but as powerful inventors; we can withdraw from the sexism around us while drawing out the best in each other; and women and men can *think* together instead of abandoning each other in anger and disappointment. We may eventually be able to step out of the cycles of history that return us to the same old problems era after era if we can learn now to think together as in a dance.

Our dreams for change are big. Our strategies must be big, too.

Most things that work are simple. And simple things lead to big changes. But we have to be willing to do these simple things, and not retreat into the comfort of 'how it has always been'. Making our work for women's empowerment into a thinking environment is just this sort of simple strategy.

One of my favourite examples from the last century is the physician Ignaz Semmelweis. In 1850, doctors (who were all male) only had to do one simple thing to save the lives of thousands of women who were dying in hospital in childbirth. They merely had to begin to wash their hands before attending a birth. But it took them fifty years to agree to do it. Today, of course, for physicians not to wash their hands between patients would be unthinkable.

But for the whole of his professional life Semmelweis had to say this simple thing over and over again to the doctors of Vienna, 'Wash your hands. That is all, just wash your hands. Throw out your self-righteous pomposity and wash your hands.' Thousands more women would die before the doctors finally agreed to do this simple thing.

We are at this kind of crossroads again. This time the simple thing we have to do is *create thinking environments together*. We have to meet together without our male-conditioned arrogance or our female-conditioned deference – and think. We will still have to demand choice, prosecute rape, keep climbing the ladders of power, change our laws, and push for all the rights and benefits women desperately need. But now women and men, as partners, also have to want new things, to explore until we find them, to have the fun of being intelligent together.

Even the fact that we are so near the destruction of the world may be an advantage. From the edge of this precipice, we can see that the way we have done things so far is not going to work. We must change or perish. We know this, and one by one, step by step, we are changing. Rarely has it been so good to be a woman or to be a man. We want change because we want life, and we know that we have never risked so much nor had so much to gain. We know it is thinking we must do and we know we must do that together. Now there is no other choice, and that may make it easier.

Thinking alongside fighting, men alongside women, joy alongside rage, appreciation alongside criticism, rest alongside work – it will take this dance to achieve women's goals. Freedom requires too much intelligence, too much grace and too much awareness ever to be achieved in a frenzy of repetitious activity. As we link our minds, we

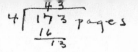

have to know exactly where we are and sense what the next step will be together. We have to respond accurately to the lives of those around us. We will turn quickly sometimes, lean gently sometimes, pause sometimes and reach out or draw in at just the right moments to stay true to our beat and to avoid obstructing the paths of others as we go. We must listen for the music, and let our ideas play it back. Without warning, we will spin and lurch and then hold each other close. And when we stumble and run into each other and the beat is lost, we can stop, remind each other, and synchronize our steps again.

Your life is yours. No one else can live it. What you do with it, from this point on, depends entirely on how well you can *think* about it. Begin the dance today. Establish a thinking environment in your life. Wonderful things can result from that simple and profound decision.

Nicci Gerrard was right. The road to permanent freedom will not be just a fight. It will also be a dance.

PART 4

Reminders

I offer this next section as a quick look at some of the principles, questions, and points in the book. Before thinking sessions and as a basis for ongoing discussion you may find these summaries helpful.

A FEW PRINCIPLES OF LEADERSHIP

1 If you have influence over even one other person, you are a leader.

2 The most important job of a leader is to create a thinking environment throughout the organization.

3 Women's culture, with its emphasis on interactive thinking skills, is a necessary training ground for leaders, especially for men.

4 The best leaders increase the amount of support in their life each time they increase the amount of leadership they take on.

5 Leading well includes being appreciated every day by the people you are leading.

6 Leaders will inspire if they lead from joy, not from duty or from the drug of frenzied drive.

7 Making mistakes is one of the requirements of good leadership.

8 Good leaders regularly review their leadership with people who can speak to them honestly, maintaining a ten to one ratio of appreciation to criticism.

9 Good leaders know everyone in their group, understand how the world has treated them and their people, and interrupt any acts, words or policies of prejudice towards them.

10 A leader's ideas can be presented in such a way that even better ideas come from others.

11 The quality of a person's public life is only as good as the quality of their solitude.

12 Leaders need at least one thinking partner who has no connection whatever with their work.

13 The art of resting deeply is essential for sound, durable leadership.

14 A leader's work will stay fresh and effective if she periodically starts from scratch and asks herself, 'What do I really want?'

15 Leadership is sometimes offered to women as a way of silencing them. Astute female leaders refuse to agree to this.

16 There is more than enough leadership opportunity to go around.

17 Effective leaders develop, celebrate and champion others in their leadership whilst never abdicating their own.

18 The best leaders bring their values with them.

19 The issues that victimize you in intimate relationships are the same issues that will victimize you in leadership.

20   When convening a meeting, an effective leader will make concrete proposals, assuming that they will be discussed and changed, rather than open the meeting by asking, 'What does everybody want to do?'

21   Thinking goes better if leaders begin each meeting or event by having *everyone* say something about themselves and end each meeting with a word from *everyone* about what has been achieved.

22   Periodically during a meeting leaders do well to stop and hear from the quiet people.

23   Our progress as women leaders can be measured not only by our political gains but also by the decreasing amount of time each day we spend as victims.

24   Good leaders listen far more than they speak.

25   Women and men grow as leaders when they allow their primary leadership role model to be a woman.

SOME RECURRING
INCISIVE QUESTIONS

1   If things could be exactly right for you in this situation, how would they be?

2   If you were not holding back in your life, what would you be doing?

3   If you were not afraid, what would you do right now?

4   What do you really want?

5   What do you really think?

6   If you were not afraid of power, how would you live differently?

7   Are you doing anything at this very moment that is building up resentment in you? If so, what could you do to prevent it?

8   If you assumed that no one could think better about this issue than you, what would you say?

9   If you knew you were the best person for the job, what would you do first?

10   What do you want to accomplish in your life before you die?

11   If you knew that someone you love very much was going to die tomorrow, what would you want to be sure to say to them today?

12   Assuming leadership is fun, what would you want to lead?

13   If a doctor told you that your life depended on putting yourself first, what would you do differently?

14 If you could trust that your children would be fine, what would you do with the rest of your life?

15 If you knew that the whole world thought you were beautiful just as you are, what would change for you?

16 If you were sure you were more intelligent than the men around you, how would you present yourself to them?

17 If you believed that crying was a process of strengthening rather than a sign of weakness, what would you cry about?

18 If you trusted that your excellence would not put others in your shadow, what would you be doing?

19 What are the changes that would turn your office into a women's culture/thinking environment?

20 If, from this moment onward, you become the *only* one who decides what happens to your body, what would have to change in your life?

THINKING INHIBITORS

Ridicule	Self-doubt
Lack of interest	Absence of appreciation
Intimidation	Rigid adherence to policy
Impatience	Formality
Interruption	An uncomfortable environment
Perfectionism	Provincialism
Cynicism	Hierarchy
Competition	Belittlement
Stereotyping	Seduction
Misinformation	Distraction
Constant criticism	Anxiety
Low expectations	Jealousy
Powerlessness	Shame

THINKING ENHANCERS

We think best when . . .

1 People pay interested, aware attention to us.
2 We think well of ourselves.
3 We know specifically how we are appreciated.
4 We trust our own thinking and insights.
5 We are encouraged to ask questions.
6 Without excessive pressure, the best is expected of us.
7 We are engaged in activity which is meaningful and in our best interests.
8 We are in charge and are not being exploited.
9 We have accurate information.
10 Our personal lives are going well.
11 Our minds are free of fear.
12 We are in active pursuit of our dreams and goals.
13 We are addressing the needs and well-being of our world.
14 We are fighting social stereotypes and prejudices.
15 We are encouraged to think beyond tradition or *status quo*.
16 We are in close, trusting, enduring relationship with others.
17 We are in an orderly, comfortable, accessible environment.
18 Our bodies are at ease.
19 Everyone in the group is given a chance to speak.
20 Our attention is on finding the best idea, not on being right.
21 Our ideas will influence a specific outcome.

Further Reading

Angelou, Maya. *And Still I Rise*. London: Virago Press, 1990.

Armstrong, Penny and Sheryl Feldman. *A Wise Birth*. New York: William Morrow and Company, 1990.

Beattie, Melody. *Codependent No More*. Harper and Row, San Francisco, 1987.

Belenky, Mary Field, Blythe McVicker Clinchy, Nancy Rule Goldberger, Jill Mattuck Tarule. *Women's Ways of Knowing*. New York: Basic Books, Inc., 1986.

Chang, Jung. *Wild Swans: Three Daughters of China*. Glasgow: HarperCollins, 1991.

Eisler, Raine. *The Chalice and the Blade*. San Francisco: Harper and Row, 1988.

Faludi, Susan. *Backlash: The Undeclared War Against American Women*. New York: Crown Publishers, 1991.

Finlay, Fergus. *Mary Robinson: A President With a Purpose*. Dublin: The O'Brien Press, Ltd., 1990.

Gilligan, Carol. *In a Different Voice*. Cambridge, Massachusetts: Harvard University Press, 1982.

Gould, Stephen Jay. *The Mismeasure of Man*. New York: W.W. Norton and Company, 1981.

Gordon, Tuula. *Feminist Mothers*. London: Macmillan Education Ltd., 1990.

Harragan, Betty Lehan. *Games Mother Never Taught You*. New York: Warner Books, 1987.

Kline, Nancy and Christopher Spence. *At Least A Hundred Principles of Love*. London: Sage Hunt Press, 1986.

Lerner, Harriet Goldhor. *The Dance of Anger.* New York: Harper and Row, 1989.

Mann, Judy. *Mann For All Seasons.* New York: MasterMedia Limited, 1990.

Miles, Rosalind. *The Women's History of the World.* London: Grafton Books, 1990. *The Rites of Man: Love, Sex, and Death in the Making of the Male.* London: Grafton Books, 1992.

Miller, Alice. *For Your Own Good.* Toronto: Collins Publishers, 1984.

Miller, Casey and Kate Swift. *Words and Women.* New York: Anchor Press/Doubleday, 1976.

Miller, Jean Baker. *Toward a New Psychology of Women.* London: Penguin Group, 1986.

Mumtaz, Khawar and Farida Shaheed, eds. *Women of Pakistan.* London: Zed Books, Ltd., 1987.

Payne, Karen. *Between Ourselves: Letters Between Mothers and Daughters.* London: Michael Joseph, Ltd., 1983.

Plato. Ed., Francis MacDonald Cornford. *The Republic of Plato.* London: Oxford University Press, 1972.

Roddick, Anita. *Body and Soul.* London: Vermillion/Random Century House, 1992.

Richardson, Diane. *Women and the AIDS Crisis.* London: Pandora Press, 1987.

Rosener, Judy. 'Ways Women Lead.' *Harvard Business Review.* Nov/Dec 1991.

Stone, Merlin. *When God Was a Woman.* London: Harcourt Brace Jovanovich, 1976.

Siegel, Bernie S. *Love, Medicine and Miracles.* New York: Harper and Row, 1986.

Steinem, Gloria. *The Revolution Within.* London: Corgi, 1992.

Tannen, Deborah. *You Just Don't Understand.* New York: Ballantine Books, 1990.

Thomas, Lewis. *The Medusa and the Snail.* New York: Bantam Books, 1979.

Thompson, Morton. *The Cry and the Covenant.* New York: Signet Books, 1955.

Walker, Alice. *Living By the Word.* London: The Women's Press Ltd., 1988.

Wolf, Naomi. *The Beauty Myth.* London: Vintage, 1991.

Index